NUMEROLOGY:
THE KEY TO YOUR INNER SELF

Richard De A'Morelli

Spectrum Ink Books

Numerology: The Key to Your Inner Self

Copyright © 1972, 2023 by Richard De A'Morelli and Spectrum Ink Books

First Printing: November 1972
Second Printing: May, 1973
Third Printing: April, 1974
Spanish Edition: June 1974
French Edition: August 1975
Fourth Printing: May 1984
Fifth Printing: May 2023

Cover image licensed from Adobe Stock Graphics. Back cover image licensed from DepositPhotos.com. Images are copyrighted by their respective owners.

All rights reserved. No part of this book may be reproduced in any form, stored in any retrieval system, or transmitted by any means, including electronic, mechanical, photocopy, recording, or otherwise without prior written permission of the publisher, except in the case of brief quotations embodied in critical reviews and certain other noncommercial uses permitted by U.S. copyright law. For permission requests, contact the publisher by email or via the Web.

Spectrum Ink Books
Email: Editor@Spectrum.org
Website: https://books.spectrum.org/
Phone: (805) 888-2900
Fax: (805) 888-2999

Retail and wholesale orders for this title in paperback, e-book, and hardcover editions may be placed using the following ISBNs. Quantity discounts are available through our global distributor, Ingram Content Group.

ISBN Numbers:
978-1-64399-016-3 : Retail Paperback (Amazon)
978-1-64399-017-0 : Wholesale Paperback (Ingram)
978-1-64399-050-7 : Hardcover (Ingram)
978-1-64399-014-9 : Amazon Kindle
978-1-64399-015-6 : EPUB (digital)

Contents

INTRODUCTION
WHAT NUMEROLOGY CAN DO FOR YOU 5

CHAPTER ONE
UNDERSTANDING THE FUNDAMENTALS 7

CHAPTER TWO
DETERMINING THE SOUL URGE 13

CHAPTER THREE
DETERMINING THE LATENT SELF 35

CHAPTER FOUR
DETERMINING THE EXPRESSIVE SELF 47

CHAPTER FIVE
DETERMINING THE LIFE PATH 55

CHAPTER SIX
DETERMINING THE KARMIC ESSENCE 71

CHAPTER SEVEN
DETERMINING THE KARMIC LESSONS 109

CHAPTER EIGHT
THE KARMIC PROJECTION TABLE 121

CHAPTER NINE
COSMIC AND PERSONAL TRENDS 173

CHAPTER TEN
PERSONAL RELATIONSHIPS 191

CHAPTER ELEVEN
THE ELEMENTS 201

CHAPTER TWELVE
SAMPLE CHART & ANALYSIS 205

CHAPTER THIRTEEN
SAMPLE PROJECTION TABLE AND ANALYSIS 215

CONCLUSION 219

Contents

INTRODUCTION
WHAT NUMEROLOGY CAN DO FOR YOU 5

CHAPTER ONE
UNDERSTANDING THE FUNDAMENTALS 7

CHAPTER TWO
DETERMINING THE SOUL URGE 13

CHAPTER THREE
DETERMINING THE LATENT SELF 35

CHAPTER FOUR
DETERMINING THE EXPRESSIVE SELF 47

CHAPTER FIVE
DETERMINING THE LIFE PATH 55

CHAPTER SIX
DETERMINING THE KARMIC ESSENCE 71

CHAPTER SEVEN
DETERMINING THE KARMIC LESSONS 109

CHAPTER EIGHT
THE KARMIC PROJECTION TABLE 121

CHAPTER NINE
COSMIC AND PERSONAL TRENDS 173

CHAPTER TEN
PERSONAL RELATIONSHIPS 191

CHAPTER ELEVEN
THE ELEMENTS 201

CHAPTER TWELVE
SAMPLE CHART & ANALYSIS 205

CHAPTER THIRTEEN
SAMPLE PROJECTION TABLE AND ANALYSIS 215

CONCLUSION 219

Introduction

What Numerology Can Do for You

Numerology has been used as a tool for divination and character analysis for more than 2,500 years. It was developed by Pythagoras, who is often called the "Father of Number." Born in Greece in 569 BC, Pythagoras was a foremost mathematician and philosopher of his time. He created the musical scale as we know it, and he invented several stringed instruments. He also discovered complex mathematical formulas, and his teachings include the doctrine: "All things in the universe are numbers."

Today, numerology is widely used in many parts of the world as a tool for character analysis, and to understand the powerful vibrations and trends at work in our daily lives. Using a person's given name at birth and date of birth, you can discover deep and amazingly accurate insights into any individual: their desires, abilities, strengths, weaknesses, even past, present, and future.

Numerology has been adapted to dozens of languages and alphabets. This handy primer is based on the English alphabet and serves as an introduction to the subject. Following the first printing of this book in 1972, it was translated into three languages, including French, Spanish, and German. It was one of the earliest, modern authoritative guides to the study of numerology, and it covered important new discoveries and developments in the field, including: the Karmic Essence Number, which can add valuable insights to a numerology chart; the Karmic Projection Table, a novel method for charting and interpreting past, present, and future trends in an individual's life; and compatibility guidelines to allow quick and easy compatibility analyses of two numerology charts.

Numerology is often called "the Science of Numbers." As Pythagoras observed, everything in the universe is governed by numbers, so in a sense, numerology, like music, is a universal language. We can listen to the well-meaning advice of family and friends, but through numerology, we can discover a multitude of valuable insights into ourselves, the myriad influences affecting us as we go about our daily living, and thus, it provides a glimpse into the course our life path will follow, and into our destiny. No other methodology is capable of such insights, and no other is as revealing or accurate.

You're skeptical? Give numerology a try. Follow the step-by-step methods outlined in this book to construct a numerology chart for yourself and for a few of our friends and family. You might be amazed by what you discover!

Chapter One

Understanding the Fundamentals

Throughout life, we are placed in situations where we must make choices. We are given free will to guide our lives toward the goals and destinations of our choosing, and we hope that each decision we make, every step we take, will be productive and beneficial. We are happy with some outcomes and disappointed with others. On those occasions in life when we run into a series of disappointing outcomes, we may question whether we really had any choice in these matters, or whether the fickle finger of fate has jinxed us.

Numerologists do not accept that life is pre-ordained and whatever happens to us is inevitable. Instead, they believe that human beings were given brains, and we were given the freedom to use our intelligence to determine our own outcomes. In other words, we have freedom of choice in all of our important undertakings, and our trivial affairs too. But there are caveats!

In numerology, we can identify and measure vibrations that will have a particular effect on our life *if we do nothing at all*. If we stand in the middle of a busy highway, no matter how many cars swerve to avoid us, sooner or later, one will run us over. But up until that very moment that we meet our "destiny," we can exercise free will and step off the highway. The moment we take that step, everything changes: where we are traveling, how we are getting there, when we will arrive, even who we are! Because, by making the conscious decision to exercise free will, we have strengthened our inner character—in that moment of decision, we have awakened an inner strength and denied the effects of inertia brought on by weaker characteristics that cause us to give in to resistance, to stop fighting for what we want, and to accept whatever lousy cards life might deal to us.

Think of numerology as a tool for discovery and empowerment. It can help you discover hidden attributes that reside within you, often without you realizing it! And it can reveal your weaker traits that set you up for failure and cause you to self-sabotage your life. These insights are enlightening and empowering. They will enable you to build on your strengths and overcome or neutralize your weaknesses, or find ways to turn them into positives.

We talk a lot about vibrations, influences, cycles, and trends in numerology. First and foremost, it is important to know that no vibrations are entirely bad, and none are wholly good. Nothing in life is that simple and clear-cut. In every positive experience lurks shadows of negativity, and if we react to our success in certain ways, those influences can disrupt our equilibrium unless we are on guard. Similarly, life's most unpleasant and painful experiences always contain in them the seeds of constructive lessons and new knowledge that we can learn if our minds are open to it.

So, when we say that a vibration is "good" or "bad," we are merely referring to its natural tendency to produce a predictable outcome if we do nothing to change it. That means, a "bad" or negative vibration can be turned into something quite good, and a "good" one can be transformed into something unpleasant or even destructive. Think back to the example of a person standing in the highway and doing nothing as cars whiz by. We will discuss many situations in this book where that metaphor applies.

As a general rule, most people are blind to these positive and negative trends and energies as they navigate through daily life. They see only what appears to be, on a superficial level, while the reality of a situation lies deeper and may not become obvious until it is too late to change course.

Numerology, often called the "Science of Numbers" and a "universal language," can reveal these unseen trends and influences we encounter in daily living. It can help us avoid obstacles and setbacks, and turn failure into success. It can provide a clearer, deeper understanding of universal laws at work in the world around us, and reveal both the positive and the negative aspects of every condition or circumstance in which we find ourselves at any moment in time. Likewise, it can alert us to potential difficulties ahead on the road of life as well as reveal positive trends we can take capitalize upon as they arise. We are no longer limited by the sole option of navigating through life on a blind course.

Every man, woman, and child alive is influenced by vibrations, or energies, which originate from many different sources, among them: human emotions (your own and the emotional energy of others), as well as manmade, environmental, and natural forces. For the sake of simplicity, in numerology, we assign numbers to these vibrations. For example, we can take the time and effort to describe "the vibration of originality, the inventor, the beginner of all things." Or, we can simply refer to the 1 vibration, and its meaning is understood.

These energies ebb and flow around us, influencing everyday affairs. They influence our actions and shape our character, our thoughts, desires, and attitudes. They fuel our hopes and dreams—and sometimes those goals conflict. A man might set out to achieve a goal that is not in his best interest, and though he knows deep down that reaching it would be destructive in the end, he continues to pursue it. We all have done this. We chalk it up to "something inside" that makes us keep going. That mysterious "something" is usually the subconscious mind, which is particularly susceptible to being influenced by the vibrations we are discussing here.

In numerology, a person has three levels of Self, and all are equally important. By learning what makes us tick on each level, and by understanding that the various personality aspects often compete with or contradict one another, we can synchronize them to work harmoniously rather than in stressful opposition.

The three levels of Self which comprise the personality are: (1) the Soul Urge, (2) the Latent Self, and (3) the Expressive Self. There are other important aspects as well, which we will discuss in later chapters of this book.

The *Soul Urge* is primarily concerned with your desires in life. Some of these desires may have been hidden or repressed since childhood, yet they are powerful urges driving your feelings and actions, often without you realizing it. These yearnings of the soul may compel a person to climb the highest mountains, or fall to the darkest depths. The Soul Urge is the underlying motivation for everything we do. By learning to understand and shape it, we can direct our lives more effectively and bring our goals to fruition.

The *Latent Self* is concerned with inborn abilities—our talents, skills, and natural abilities. Not everyone is endowed with the same skills or can succeed in the same areas. Some individuals may have a natural inclination to pursue art, writing, or drama; others might be skilled carpenters or craftsmen, while yet others gravitate into careers as doctors, scientists, or educators. No matter what natural abilities you possess, within you lies the potential for greatness. If you do not pursue and achieve it, you'll short-change yourself in life and likely become restless, dissatisfied, or altogether miserable. Likewise, the opposite holds true—if a person strives to reach goals beyond their capabilities, they may achieve only limited success or utterly fail. Thus, understanding the Latent Self is an essential part of the equation for navigating a path to success and happiness.

The *Expressive Self* is the third personality aspect we are covering in this introduction, and it is a mix of your desires and capabilities. It reflects what you are actually doing in life. As you might guess, this can be a source of conflict in a numerology chart. What you are doing might not sync with what you want to do, or what you are capable of doing. When your desires (Soul Urge) and your abilities (Latent Self) are out of sync or in conflict, the result is often chaotic, and your life may be awash in stress, discord, and unhappiness.

Numerology can provide you with surprisingly accurate insights into these three personality aspects. Once you've identified your desires, abilities, and current actions in daily living, you'll be better able to pinpoint and navigate around pitfalls and obstacles you encounter on the road of life. You can channel your positive energy and harmonize these three aspects of personality so that they work in sync, and so that your thoughts and actions lead to worthwhile accomplishments.

A fourth aspect that holds weight in numerology is the *Karmic Essence* vibration. It represents the combined effect or culmination of the Soul Urge, Latent Self, and Expressive Self, revealing a composite of you. By analyzing this vibration, you can pinpoint more precisely where you are in life and how to reach the goals and outcomes that you desire.

Various other insights can be gleaned using the time-honored principles of numerology. You can analyze the pros and cons of friendships, romances, and business partnerships, with remarkable accuracy. Numerology allows you to identify and analyze the underlying trends and forces at work in your life at any given time.

Another highly useful tool in the numerologist's arsenal, discussed later in this book, is the *Karmic Projection Table*. Using this advanced charting technique, you can pinpoint and interpret past, present, and future vibrations at work in a person's life from year to year. These valuable insights can help you know when to change and what changes to make. You can identify the most and least favorable times to pursue material, emotional, and spiritual goals in life. You can discover the particular vibrations affecting your life at any particular time and how powerful they will be.

If, for example, you know that the vibration of physical strain, compromised health, and being accident-prone is strong in a particular year of your life, you can make conscious decisions and take actions to minimize your risk and maintain good health and vitality, while those who ignore the prevailing vibrations in their charts will be more apt to encounter difficulties.

As previously mentioned, numerology does not accept the premise that fate controls your life or events are pre-destined. You are the master of your life and destiny; numerology brings signposts into focus that you can follow as you travel the road of life. Always, in all matters, you have free will and freedom of choice. Knowing what lies ahead or at least being able to identify the numerological vibrations in play will enable you to flow with the tide of the universe rather than struggling upstream. As the saying goes, you can plant roses in your spiritual garden rather than filling it with bitter herbs.

As you read through this book and learn to calculate numerology charts for yourself and others, remember that just as you have power over your destiny, no rule in numerology is ever set in stone. Interpretations are intended as general guidelines, and as your understanding of numerology grows, so will your understanding of the subtle nuances you detect in the charts that you analyze.

Life is a churning, ever-changing vortex of invisible energies that ebb and flow, sometimes moving you forward, other times holding you back. But you are the captain of your ship and the master of your fate. We can look to numerology much as we would review a weather forecast predicting conditions in the atmosphere. It can help us navigate through the complexities of life and ensure that we are in sync with the universe.

Begin your journey into numerology by calculating your own chart using this handbook as a guide, and you will quickly recognize the valuable and intriguing insights that the Science of Numbers can reveal.

Chapter Two

Determining the Soul Urge

The vowels in your name reveal your Soul Urge. We determine this value by assigning numbers to each vowel in your first, middle, and last name at birth, and then we add those values together. We will work through an example below.

Every syllable in a name should have at least one vowel. The vowels in English are: A, E, I, O, U, and sometimes Y, as explained in the next paragraph. All other letters in the name are consonants.

Treat "Y" as a vowel if it is the only vowel in a syllable. For example, it is a vowel in Mary, Tyler, and Dorothy – because "y" (shown in bold) is the only possible vowel in the syllable:

Mar-**y**

T**y**-ler

Dor-o-th**y**

In the names below, however, "y" is a consonant because the syllable in which it appears has another vowel (shown in bold):

Ca-s**e**y

Ash-l**e**y

W**a**yne

There's an exception to the rule that every syllable must have a vowel. Rarely, a child will be given a birthname with no vowel, such as JJ. Here, the vowel total would be zero. Calculate the rest of the name as explained in this chapter to find the Soul Urge.

Every letter in a person's first, middle, and last name—vowels as well as consonants—has a number value, shown in this table:

1	2	3	4	5	6	7	8	9
A	B	C	D	E	F	G	H	I
J	K	L	M	N	O	P	Q	R
S	T	U	V	W	X	Y	Z	

To determine your Soul Urge, add the vowels in the first name and reduce the total to a single digit, 1 through 9. By "reduce," we mean add the digits of the number together. So, if the sum of the letters in the first name is 26, you would reduce: 2 + 6 = 8.

Do the same for the middle and last name.

Now, add the three totals together and reduce to a value of 19 or less, or 22. So, if the sum of the three numbers is 26, you would reduce: 2 + 6 = 8. Or, if the sum of the three numbers is 16, do not reduce further since the result is 19 or less.

Here is an example using the fictitious name Daniel John Sutter: First, write down the name and locate the vowels. Then, assign the number value from the table above to each vowel:

```
D A N I E L   J O H N   S U T T E R
  1   9 5       6         3     5
```

Add up all the vowels in the first name and reduce the total to a single digit. So, for the first name, we add 1 + 9 + 5 = 15; and then reduce to a single digit: 1 + 5 = 6.

Repeat this step for the middle name and last name, which will give you three single-digit totals: 6 | 6 | 8.

Now, add these three single-digit totals together, and follow the special rule to reduce to 19 or less, or the number 22.

```
DANIEL      6

JOHN        6

SUTTER      8
```

Add the three single-digit totals together:

6 + 6 + 8 = 20

Reduce until the result is 19 or less, or the number 22.

2 + 0 = 2

This tells us that Daniel's Soul Urge is 2.

Assume that the three name values had been 8 + 6 + 8. The total is 22 so do not reduce. If the totals had been 4 + 4 + 8 = 16, don't reduce because the sum is 19 or less, or 22. The final total reveals the Soul Urge.

Remember, you must use a person's full name at birth to build a numerology chart, and the spelling of the full name must be exactly as it appears on the person's birth certificate. And always doublecheck your calculations. One small error can seriously undermine the accuracy of a chart.

To find the meaning of the Soul Urge vibration, refer to the numbers in the interpretation guide below.

Guide to the Soul Urge

1

You are daring and pioneering; always searching for the new and unexplored. You yearn to be creative.

You have a great deal of inner drive and forcefulness. Because of those qualities and your desire for constant action and progress, you would make a strong leader.

You have a good head on your shoulders and want to be left unhampered to carry out your plans and ideas.

You continually strive to change and expand, but you sometimes get bogged down, and all your energies do little good as you spin your wheels and get nowhere.

You are brimming with energy and bubbling over with rare enthusiasm. You are anxious to tackle life in all its intricate details.

It is difficult for you to remain static and unmoving, and often, you may find yourself restless and bored.

Your strong will and positivity can make you a power for good.

2

You are at your best when surrounded by an atmosphere of peace and harmony.

You want to enjoy the luxuries of life, but you never make unreasonable demands to obtain them.

You want peace and harmony in your surroundings, regardless of the cost to yourself. You go to great extremes and make painful sacrifices to keep close friends and loved ones happy.

You are not particularly business-minded, and you are not concerned with accumulating vast sums of money, fame, or power over other people. In fact, you tend to shy away from conditions which could bring this about for you.

You are content with the small things in life, and although you are intrigued by glamour, you do not struggle to attain it.

You find it easy enough to be cheerful and happy no matter where you are or how difficult your circumstances may be.

You often have trouble exercising discipline over children or younger loved ones. Your desire to keep peace and good cheer in your family and home prevents you from applying a stern hand.

You are easy to get along with, and you want many friends from all walks of life. You avoid making enemies at all costs.

One of your best assets is loyalty. In love, you are faithful even if you must overlook infidelity in others.

You are kind, sympathetic, gentle, and compassionate. Being understanding comes naturally to you.

You want to reach out and comfort those who suffer, and you tend to experience the same pain they do when you are with them.

Most people consider you soft-hearted. You hardly ever insist on having your own way.

Many people come to you with their problems. They know you can keep a secret, and they have full trust in you.

3

You have a strong inclination towards art and creativity.

You are naturally talented and may consider pursuing a career in music, writing, theatre, painting, or another artistic venue.

You don't let discouragement get you down. You laugh at failure and simply try again.

You are high-spirited and enthusiastic.

You don't allow worry to get the best of you, and you live day-to-day, believing that everything will take care of itself in due time.

You are very bright, highly inspired, and talented in areas where your vivid imagination and creativity can be put to good use.

You are friendly and outgoing. You crave friends, praise, and popularity. Throughout life, you'll maintain a wide range of social contacts, especially people who are successful in creative fields such as writing, music, art, or drama.

You are well-liked and rarely encounter problems interacting with other people. You have the unique ability to get along with practically anyone.

You consider life a game, and it's always easy for you to find amusement.

Friends and family may often get upset with you because you find it difficult to be too serious. Your attitude is that everyone lives only once, so you might as well enjoy the journey.

You may be involved in social movements since you desire world improvement, but nothing will hold your attention for very long. You will tend to move from one thing to another, embracing each experience to the fullest before moving on to the next.

4

Under this vibration, you are practical and patient.

You are dependable and make a point of being on time for business meetings, interviews, and appointments. You expect the same courtesy from others.

You try to remain organized at all times, for you know nothing can be accomplished in the midst of chaos.

You lead an ideal life as far as you are concerned: you are dignified, poised, and conservative.

You would not make a particularly good leader under this vibration because you prefer having someone else direct. However, you only need to be shown once, and then you know the details of any job or task perfectly.

You are warm and loving, but you can be difficult to understand. You are not very demonstrative when it comes to affection, although you would do practically anything to protect your loved ones and friends.

You are loyal and trustworthy. Cheating is not your style, and you do not like to see others resort to unfair tactics or take advantage of people who are less fortunate.

You avoid rash and impulsive actions, but because of this, you sometimes fall into a rut. This is because you resist changing your old ways and prefer to stick to routines. You find security in familiarity and prefer things to stay the way they always have been.

You desire affection, but you can come across as cool and aloof. You are not excessively affectionate, and you may seem detached compared to natives of more passionate vibrations. However, individuals with a 4 Soul Urge make some of the most devoted, loyal, and trustworthy marriage partners.

You have a great deal of energy and can easily dedicate yourself to any task, working tirelessly until the desired outcome is achieved.

You appreciate honesty, and you despise lying.

You are thrifty and frugal, and you never squander your funds because you understand how much effort and hard work it takes to earn money. You appreciate the value of a dollar.

5

The most important thing in life to you is maintaining your independence and personal freedom. You do not want to be tied down, and you avoid commitment whenever possible.

You want to think your own thoughts and discover your own truths without interference from friends or family.

You never find yourself bored or stuck in a rut. You dislike routine and must constantly be on the go traveling, meeting new people, and visiting new places. In general, you seek a good time.

You enjoy being unconventional, and it amuses you when others consider you strange or eccentric.

Loyalty is not one of your strong suits, and you tend to discard old friends without much thought.

In love, you often find yourself unhappy because you cannot remain interested in one person for any extended period of time.

You are fun to be around. People seek you out and appreciate your enthusiastic approach to life.

You find excitement in everything that is new and different, and you will be involved in many unusual adventures during your life, some of which may not be beneficial to you.

You are resilient, resourceful, and always bounce back quickly from problems, diving back into the swing of things with renewed enthusiasm. You believe that where there's a will, there's a way.

6

You desire a happy home and family, beauty in your surroundings, a devoted lover or life partner, affection, and happiness above all else in life.

You willingly shoulder more than your fair share of responsibility, and you do it cheerfully and without complaint.

You are a loyal friend and a good counselor. People often seek you out for help with their problems. You give of yourself freely.

You are overly protective of your friends and family. You would rather get hurt in their place than see them suffer.

You are kind, sympathetic, and understanding. Among all the vibrations, you make the best romantic or life partner because you are willing and able to make the necessary adjustments required in a deep and lasting relationship.

You are stable and well-balanced. You have good judgment, a keen sense of fair play, and you are often asked to help negotiate peace in disputes among family and friends.

Sometimes, you tend to be a martyr for your loved ones or your ideals. Most of the suffering and angst that you experience in life is brought on by your desire to be helpful and your unwavering trust and confidence in those who show you attention or affection.

7

This is the vibration of analysis.

You have a scientific mind and analyze problems from every

angle before arriving at a conclusion. This scientific approach often annoys your friends.

The 7 Soul Urge often sparks a keen interest in religion, philosophy, and spirituality.

You have strong, natural psychic abilities. You should learn to harness your abilities for the betterment of humanity.

You are quiet, introverted, but filled with wisdom.

You are a skilled debater, and you usually have the final say. In arguments, you are nearly always correct because you know what you're talking about before you speak. You come straight to the point, leaving little room for further discussion.

Some people find you difficult to understand or get close to because you tend to be withdrawn and secretive.

8

Success, wealth, and leadership are the focus of the 8, known as the vibration of Material Mastery. You desire power and the freedom to launch new businesses and generate money on a large scale.

You may find it difficult to work under superiors, and you would do best running your own business or serving in a senior-management capacity.

You are strong in organization, and you are a good manager, but you often scatter your energies trying to do to many jobs at once in your haste to achieve accomplishments.

You have a practical mind, are grounded in reality and common sense, and it is almost impossible to deceive you.

Although you have a down-to-earth sense about money, your emotions and love life are likely to be rather erratic. You are more inclined towards physical relationships than intimate encounters.

You are self-reliant and value your independence. You do not like having to depend on others.

If you apply yourself in positive ways and remain ethical, you are certain to succeed.

9

Depth, sensitivity, and spirituality are highlighted under this vibration. Numerologists refer to this as the "finishing vibration," and those who believe in reincarnation see the 9 vibration as representing an old soul.

You desire personal love and happiness, but deep down, you worry that you may never attain them. You feel a sense of belonging to the universe and no one person can possess you.

You cannot resist helping those in need, and you cannot sit by while someone suffers.

In your zeal to assist others, you often give more of yourself than you should. Consequently, you may find yourself drained and sometimes depressed. You believe that you have unlimited energy and sometimes spread yourself too thin.

You are sympathetic and compassionate. You are endowed with qualities from all the lower vibrations (1-8), enabling you to be of greater service to those who need you.

You are spiritual and intuitive. You will have many hunches and premonitions in life, and they are usually accurate.

You will have many loves throughout life, but few if any will be able to tie you down for very long. There will always be something or someone demanding your attention, and you are willing to sacrifice everything if the need is great enough.

You tend to act impulsively and lack good judgment at times, even though you strive to be practical and analytical.

10

(See Number 1)

11

This is the vibration of psychic awareness. Most people with an 11 Soul Urge have a fascination with all things psychic or metaphysical. You are probably a gifted psychic. You will have many hunches and premonitions throughout life.

You are deeply interested in spiritual matters, but some of your beliefs may be unconventional. You may gravitate toward offbeat religions or philosophies. However, it is important to keep one foot anchored in reality.

You possess a great amount of unexpressed power.

You consider yourself emotionally intense and passionate, and at times, you are. But you also keep a part of yourself above the chaotic conditions of the world, which may lead some people to perceive you as detached and aloof.

You have a thirst for knowledge and aim to accumulate as much knowledge and life experience as you can. You seek ways to share your wisdom for the betterment of humanity.

You have a reformer streak and a desire to make the world a better place. You find it challenging at times to relate to human needs on an intimate level. You have an excellent grasp of universal concepts, but you sometimes put your beliefs above the feelings of others, which can lead to misunderstandings and animosity.

People often come to you for help, and you try to provide them with insightful and useful solutions. You would make a good counselor, although you tend to become overly involved in the affairs of others, and you are deeply affected when someone you are trying to help stumbles or fails.

Your love life may not be fulfilling because romance typically is typically not your top priority. Your partner may feel ignored or left out of your plans, leading to friction and quarrels.

You often view new acquaintances and strangers you've just met as friends, and your overly trusting nature can sometimes lead you into situations that you regret.

You tend to be a martyr, and you willingly defend unconventional causes. However, you must be cautious not to trust blindly, and avoid being deceived or misled astray by unscrupulous people.

Throughout life, you will have a few close friends and many acquaintances. The people you are drawn to will share similar interests, and you will meet them on common ground.

You have many pet causes that you are passionate about, and you will work tirelessly to bring them into action.

You are generally dissatisfied with the state of the world and strive to improve the conditions under which humanity lives.

12

Under this vibration, you are original, artistic, and creative. It combines the individuality of the 1 primary vibration and the harmonious temperament of the 2 with the underlying urge for creativity and artistic self-expression associated with the 3.

You tend to worry too much, and while you have many great ideas, you have trouble following through on them, so you spin your wheels and make little progress.

When things don't go as expected, you don't react well to disappointment. Sometimes you take this reaction to the extreme and you become bitter and withdrawn.

In emotional relationships, you are gentle, warm, and giving. You focus all your attention on your partner and you don't usually vacillate. You strive to be dependable, although you may be prone to telling white lies to spare someone's feelings.

You spend quite a bit of time worrying about yourself, your physical appearance, your needs and wants, and the general condition of your life.

Some people with this Soul Urge are prone to exaggerating the truth to gain attention, so it would be beneficial to learn how to use your love of drama and flair for storytelling in constructive ways.

Although you have many positive characteristics, you often have deep misgivings about your own abilities and may sometimes believe that you are useless or destined to failure.

It is important to strive for open and positive expression of your feelings, which will allow your inner beauty to shine through. You'll be pleased with the positive reactions from others around you.

13

With the 13 vibration, you are loyal and possess tremendous endurance. You embody the individuality of the 1 vibration and the creativity of the 3 built on a foundation of practicality and stability from the underlying 4 vibration.

You direct your energies efficiently, and once you set your mind on a goal, you won't stop working until you achieve results.

You yearn for change and new experiences, but you also fear the unknown and are apprehensive about the future, so you often resist change, even when you know it is in your best interest.

You are prone to getting stuck in a rut and find security in routine. Despite your calm and dependable façade, you can be insecure. You crave recognition and work tirelessly to earn it.

Some of your friends perceive you as dull because you can seem overly practical, narrow-minded, and rigid in your views.

You view the world as strictly black and white. It would benefit you to learn that there are shades of gray as your friends often point out.

You possess a deeply ingrained sense of right and wrong. But you sometimes forget that your views and values are not universal laws, and others are entitled to their beliefs. Your opinionated and argumentative nature can cause relationships to become strained or break down altogether.

You often handle touchy situations clumsily.

Love and affection are important to you, and you invest a lot of energy in pursuing them. However, you are not entirely comfortable with intimacy, and you avoid getting too close.

Loyalty is one of your best attributes. In all your relationships with friends, business colleagues, and romantic partners, you try very hard to be fair, trustworthy, and honest.

You are rarely flirtatious, but you have a jealous streak and can be quite possessive.

You have a temper that flairs up during arguments. It would be beneficial for you to learn to control the urge to lash out with harsh words and be less judgmental.

14

You are very intelligent, perhaps brilliant, and you can achieve great success under the 14 vibration.

You value personal freedom so highly that you sometimes obstinately pursue it to the point of being irresponsible.

You have issues with responsibility and tend to resist taking the blame for the consequences of your actions.

You often make rash decisions and have hurt yourself in the past by foolish actions that you know are wrong but you pursue them anyway. However, at times, you procrastinate endlessly, swinging back and forth between extremes.

It is important to choose your friends wisely, because you are not a good judge of character and may attract dishonest or unscrupulous people who take advantage of you.

Friends find it difficult to understand you, and some perceive you as a thrill-seeker or selfish because you insist on doing what you want.

When making life decisions, you instinctively know what is right for you, but sometimes fail to choose the best course of action out of fear that it will lead to a dull, plodding, or routine existence.

Guard against careless outbursts of temper when arguing your opinions. You have lost friends over your angry words and actions.

In your quest for freedom, you find it difficult to settle down in one romantic relationship for very long.

You are drawn to sensuality and may easily become addicted to physical stimuli. Many natives of this Soul Urge go through a period in life where they experiment with drugs, sex, or alcohol. Be careful, as clinging to physical sensation can be your undoing.

Throughout life, you will be drawn to new and unconventional philosophies and offbeat lifestyles.

15

You want love, a happy home, roots, and security.

Love is essential to you, and without it, you are miserable.

You are sympathetic and understanding, but you often care for the wrong people, and they use or abuse you.

You find pet causes that pull on your heart strings and work tirelessly to support them.

You are likely to have musical talents, or you love music, and you have a fondness for natural beauty.

Quite a few people who share this vibration pursue careers in acting, theater, or photography with a strong likelihood of success.

You stress out about small matters and waste too much time worrying about things over which you have little or no control.

You should pay more attention to your own affairs and take less interest in the affairs and day-to-day dramas of others.

Suspicion, jealousy, and possessiveness are weak points for you. Because you invest so much of yourself into your relationships, you are fearful of losing their love or being abandoned.

You are highly sensitive and moody, which makes you prone to bouts of anxiety and depression.

You will make a good partner in marriage because you are kind, generous, affectionate, and cooperative. You understand the necessary adjustments required in an intimate relationship.

16

You are intelligent, sensitive, spiritual, and deeply emotional, but you have a practical side. You can be an extremist, swinging back and forth between daydreams and cold reality.

You crave intimacy and the closeness of a gratifying love relationship. You fall in love quickly and love deeply.

There's a good chance that at least a few of your past relationships have involved co-dependency. Your friends advise you to avoid these relationships because they are unhealthy for you, but you love to be needed and you crave affection, so you go to great lengths to find it.

You have frequent mood swings, which can lead to bouts of instability and depression. You should take up meditation or other methods of balancing your emotions, and you'll be much happier when you do.

When you are not being overly emotional, you have common sense and a practical head on your shoulders. The trick is remembering to use it.

You may at times feel that life is not worth living if you don't have someone to love. This may lead you to fall for unsuitable partners, and there's an inherent risk of becoming involved in abusive relationships, especially before age 32. The sooner you discard the notion that being in a bad relationship is better than having no relationship at all, the better off you will be.

Throughout life, you'll have many hunches and premonitions. You should listen to your inner voice, as your intuitive feelings are usually right.

Between your intuition and keen powers of observation, you are very aware of what is going on around you. Nothing slips by you unnoticed—although you sometimes choose not to mention your discoveries.

You spend a lot of time going through the various stages of introspection and self-examination. You are deeply spiritual, and your strong views about life and the universe help to keep your mind in a good place.

You can be quite fickle, and you often have trouble making up your mind, especially in affairs of the heart.

Friends and family may find it difficult dealing with your mood swings. One minute, you can be cold, aloof, critical, and petty; the next, you can be warm, compassionate, and affectionate, depending on what is going on in your life at that moment.

You can be secretive and not always honest in relationships. You rationalize that it's better to keep secrets than to hurt others with the truth. But sometimes you just want to avoid confrontation or inconvenience to yourself.

You can be jealous and possessive, but you don't like those qualities in a lover. But more than a few of your love interests will harbor those feelings because you can behave unpredictably and give your partners good reason to feel insecure.

Of all the vibrations, 16 is the most prone to nervous anxiety, moodiness, and depression. Guard against these emotions, as they can have a corrosive effect on your cherished relationships you don't want to lose.

17

Under this vibration, you are a born leader.

You are strong-willed, resourceful, and capable of handling major problems as they arise. But the small issues in daily life often trip you up and may seem unsolvable problems.

You channel all of your energy into reaching your life goals, but in the process, you overwork yourself to exhaustion, and you are too drained to enjoy the fruits of your labors.

You are organized and efficient, but not always dependable.

You insist on being recognized for your abilities and accomplishments, and you respond well to praise. You don't like being ignored, and you intensely dislike being used or taken for granted.

You will craft numerous get-rich-quick schemes, but they rarely pan out because you don't put enough thought or effort into these ideas or think them through to logical conclusions.

You can be impatient. You don't like having to wait for the results of your hard work to materialize. You want to see your achievements rewarded instantly.

You tend to be just as impatient with your friends, colleagues at work, and family. You expect them to live up to your standards, which often sets you up for disappointment because most people are not as focused or driven as you are.

You must guard against narrow-mindedness, intolerance, and being oppressively judgmental or you will alienate people whose support you need to achieve your most important life goals.

18

Throughout life, you'll be faced with many difficult or complex choices, and you'll envy the comparatively simple lives that others around you seem to lead. The 18 combines the originality of the 1 vibration with the material success and prosperity of the 8, but reduces (1 + 8) to a 9, often called the "finishing" vibration and associated with universal service.

You are quite sentimental and sometimes go overboard with your emotions. You are generous to a fault and far too trusting for your own good. You must learn not to accept everything at face value to avoid continually setting yourself up for disappointment.

Your love life will take unexpected twists and turns. You may yearn for intimacy and struggle to achieve it, but deep down, you know that your purpose in life will require you to focus the bulk of your time and energy outside your home.

This vibration favors travel, both for business and pleasure. You are likely to have several major moves in life that will require you to leave friends, family, and familiar places behind.

One of the main pitfalls under this vibration is wasting energy. Even when you know that chasing a goal will be unproductive, you move forward stubbornly, trying to accomplish the impossible.

You can be fickle and sarcastic. Your propensity to say what you think may leave family and friends with hurt feelings.

Guard against becoming bitter, cynical, or morose.

19

This is a challenging vibration. Some numerologists view the 19 as an indicator of a karmic debt or abuse of power in a past life that must now be settled. Something was taken from the universe that was not earned, and the debt must now be paid. Others believe it reflects a "misuse of power" challenge one will encounter at some point in the here and now and which must be overcome. Yet another view is that the 19 is an unwieldy mix of fresh beginnings (from the 1) and endings (from the 9), which sets up a fundamental contradiction. Since it reduces (1 + 9) to 1, some interpret it as a phoenix rising from the ashes—new forest growth kindled by a raging inferno which seemingly destroys the forest but restarts the life cycle anew.

The 19 vibration typically signals sudden change, sporadic progress, and unexpected delays. Plans surge forward and stall just as suddenly. Some goals are achieved with unexpected ease; others remain so persistently elusive that a person eventually gives up and changes direction.

You will be given choices throughout life that require great reflection and discernment. You must make the right choices and avoid straying into any circumstance that hints of a misuse of power—shady business dealings, fraudulent transactions, forging a college degree on a resume, and so on. For the most part, the downside that attaches to the 19 vibration can be avoided if one makes wise choices and pursues constructive goals in life.

Expressed in its most positive form, the root 1 vibration will impart courage and individuality, while the 9 brings a mission of universal service through which great good can be accomplished in your community or the world. You can succeed in a wide range of vocations, from inventor and entrepreneur (the 1) to minister, counselor, teacher, and scientist (the 9).

You will be given opportunities to wield power and influence, and you will be required to choose how you will use that power for positive or negative ends. Thus, you set your course to ascend to the loftiest heights or plumb the darkest depths in your life. You are the maker of your destiny. Walking this path means that you have attained an intellectual and spiritual maturity which requires you to think for yourself and take responsibility for your actions.

22

This Soul Urge is the "Master Vibration," and it represents an innate desire for material and spiritual mastery. You will want to develop your talents and skills to the highest possible degree and put them to good use in life. You are motivated, resourceful, industrious, and down-to-earth. You'll be given many opportunities for success in life, and the only thing that will stand in your way is you!

Under this vibration, you are practical in material endeavors. But you can be demanding and judgmental. You will likely have unrealistic expectations in friendships and romances.

You strive to be organized and dependable, and you maintain a cool, calm, and collected facade. Others see you as a pillar of strength, and many people will depend on you to move projects forward and to achieve results.

You have definite ideas on how you want to conduct your life, and you set high standards for yourself. At the same time, you are flexible and pragmatic, and you can adjust course when necessary, adapting to any condition in which you find yourself.

You see yourself as the master of all crafts, the source of all knowledge for those in need, and the captain of the ship entrusted with the responsibility for completing the journey and bringing the fleet safely back to port.

You want to experience the excitement of life where calculated risks are required and you revel in outsmarting your adversaries and competitors. You want to build great things for lasting benefit, but beware of distorted idealism, which can be your downfall.

Chapter Three

Determining the Latent Self

The second aspect of personality analysis that we'll will consider in numerology is the Latent Self. It reveals a person's inborn talents and abilities. As you might guess, our desires (Soul Urge) and abilities (Latent Self) won't always be in accord and could even compete or conflict. When we observe such conflicts in a chart, we almost always find them in a person's daily life as well. Thus, numerology gives us a way to pinpoint our desires and abilities, and bring them into sync so that they work together rather than pull us in conflicting directions.

The Latent Self is determined from the *consonants* in the first, middle and last name at birth. We follow the same procedure as we did earlier, using vowels to calculate the Soul Urge. First, we assign the corresponding number value to each consonant, and then, we follow the rules given previously to reduce the sum of the three names to a final value of 19 or less, or 22.

Here is an example of how to calculate the Latent Self, using the same name as we did previously for the Soul Urge:

```
DANIEL    JOHN     SUTTER
4 5   3   1 8 5    1 2 2 9
```

Add the consonants in the first name and reduce:

4 + 5 + 3 = 12 | 1 + 2 = 3

Add the consonants in the middle name and reduce:

1 + 8 + 5 = 14 | 1 + 4 = 5

Now add the consonants in the last name and reduce:

1 + 2 + 2 + 9 = 14 | 1 + 4 = 5

Finally, add the three numbers derived from the first middle, and last name, and then reduce to 19 or less, or 22.

    D A N I E L   3

    J O H N   5

    S U T T E R   5

In this example, the Latent Self vibration is:

3 + 5 + 5 = 13

To understand the meaning of the Latent Self vibrations, refer to the interpretation guide below.

Guide to the Latent Self

1

You can go all the way to the top in life! Don't be content to settle for second place or you will never be happy. You've got to be number one, the best, and you have the ability to get there. This vibration is imaginative and original. Inventors, scientists, doctors, researchers, real estate developers, and innovators in various fields are often born with this Latent Self vibration. You have a knack for starting businesses, initiating projects, pushing forward ideas, and improving conditions. Pay close attention to following through with details.

2

You have a cooperative, harmonious disposition and get along well with almost anyone. You are a team player and deeply concerned with the human condition. Social workers, teachers, counselors, psychologists, and EMT medics commonly share this vibration. You concern yourself with the conditions affecting life and don't like to see other people suffer.

You are not obsessed with making a great name for yourself or amassing tremendous wealth. Rather, you are content working in essential roles, tending to the needs of others, and helping people who are less fortunate than yourself. You can work well with younger children, and you will be happiest in a position that allows you freedom and the ability to enact social programs or necessary changes to benefit others.

3

You are artistic and creative. You have the ability to express your talents through any creative medium such as art, writing, music, or drama. You have an inborn dramatic quality that makes you good in whatever line of work you choose, but you would excel in a vocation where you can express your creativity. You have a strong need for appreciation, and you want to be given credit for your achievements. Without ample encouragement, you'll quickly lose interest in an endeavor.

4

You are strong on organization, but you are not particularly motivated to pursue leadership roles. You have energy and drive, and you will work tirelessly for any cause or goal if you believe in the end result. You are efficient, productive, dependable; a hard worker and a loyal employee. You are admired by your colleagues and superiors. You do not like to cause trouble, and you don't like others who do so.

Natives under the 4 Latent Self have an affinity for science, medicine, technology, and machinery. They would do well as pharmacists, technicians, mechanics, lab technicians, paramedics, and first responders. Other careers suited to this vibration include fashion designers, architects, builders, craftsmen, government workers, administrators, and accountants.

5

Travel and adventure are likely under this vibration. The 5 Latent Self favors professions that involve glamour, fashion, travel, advertising, marketing, and socializing. Pilots, flight and cruise attendants, travel agents and tour guides are a good fit here, as are party planners, models, photographers, talk or game show hosts, or other vocations that require an outgoing personality. Those ruled by the 5 vibration are not especially concerned with amassing a fortune and are more interested in freedom, adventure, and enjoying life to the fullest. If this is your vibration, you would be happiest in a vocation where you can travel the world or mingle in exotic settings with people from all strata of society and walks of life. You have an extroverted personality that you can develop, if you have not already done so, and you can make it work to your advantage. Don't allow yourself to be limited by tradition and mundane responsibilities. When making a career move, think outside the box and make a concerted effort to find a job that you'll find both challenging and exciting.

6

The 6 vibration's focus is on love, family, home life, and emotional happiness. You have an excellent understanding of human relationships, and you would do well in any occupation where you can share your insights into the human experience to benefit others. A marriage counselor, wedding planner, caregiver, nurse, or therapist would be good choices for an individual with this Latent Self vibration. You enjoy nature, parks, spectacular scenery, long walks, and rainy days. You would do well in any profession that puts you out in nature. You are a romantic at heart and not terribly concerned with making lots of money or getting ahead in the world. You want to be comfortable and happy. You would be content as a stay-at-home parent or in any job where you are working with children. You would be just as happy dropping out of the rat race and living off the grid.

7

This Latent Self vibration indicates a sharp, analytical mind and wisdom in full bloom. You should choose a profession in which you can learn about life on all levels and help others learn as well. Not all of the lessons you learn will be pleasant, but you will make the most of opportunities as they arise, finding rewards where you can. You have natural empathy and a caring disposition, but you manage to stay cool and detached, making you a good candidate for any profession where you are working with people in need; for example, in caregiving, therapy, and other support roles. You are insightful and possess an astute understanding of human nature. People often come to you for advice, and you manage to offer truly inspired guidance most of the time.

You have a keen sense of attention to detail and an analytical mind, which are among your strong attributes. This vibration is also associated with religion, and you might be inclined to pursue a church-related job or occupation that involves sociology, teaching, or scientific research, where you can put your sharp mind to work. The 7 vibration hints at the possibility of fame and public recognition, but you will be happiest when you shy away from the limelight. You are resourceful and have the will-power and temperament to overcome all obstacles.

8

You have natural leadership capabilities. You are good with money, adept at planning and organizing, and you are a builder.

As a profession, you might try your hand at building anything from houses to a business empire, and you are capable of going all the way to the top. You have a good grasp of business, law, and finance, and you could succeed as an entrepreneur, a small business owner, corporate executive, lawyer, or politician. You will be happiest surrounded by the buzz of business and commerce, planning new projects, evaluating business proposals, starting companies, or immersing yourself in the various professions favored under this vibration. You might not enjoy financial wrangling, but you have a knack for it, and you can drive a terrific deal. Provided that you channel your energies into positive endeavors and avoid procrastinating, you will likely find yourself in positions where you can amass fame and wealth. Don't be content dwelling on trivial issues in life—you are capable of much more than that!

9

This is the vibration of universality. You want roots, a family and love—if you are lucky, life might give you a taste of that, but your mission is serving the world. You are kind and sympathetic, a good counselor or psychologist. You can move mountains and change the world if you avoid self-pity and don't succumb to melancholy. Any kind of work that allows you to be in close contact with people, providing advice or solutions to their problems, will put you on a trajectory to success.

In life, you will find many people come to you with their problems. You often amaze your friends and colleagues because you are insightful, brimming with energy, and you stubbornly persevere. You are prone to become discouraged and throw your hands up in despair occasionally, but you should always remember that the answer to every problem can be found if you earnestly search for it. You were born with deep spiritual discernment—use it to help others and to ensure your own path to success and a fulfilling life.

10

(See Number One)

11

Under the 11 vibration, you will be best-suited to professions in the areas of social welfare, counseling, religion, politics, and occupations concerned with justice and social change, such as politics, advocacy, journalism, broadcast news, law, and the non-profit sector. You are intuitive, spiritual, and have a great deal of empathy. You want everything in life to be fair. Injustice, even to strangers, greatly upsets you. You often get involved in the problems of other people, and you are eager to help. Sometimes, you may be drawn into shady dealings because you are too quick to trust and believe that everyone has seeds of good in them. Your family and friends sometimes worry about you being naïve, and their worries are probably justified.

You have the potential for leadership, particularly in social or reform movements. You'll find yourself placed in positions where you must make decisions of monumental importance that will affect the lives and fortunes of many. You are conscientious and always put forth your best effort. Never mope over mistakes.

12

You are not shy, but you are not especially open with your feelings, and sometimes you have trouble expressing yourself. You would find fulfilling work opportunities in any creative field, once you learn to open up and let your feelings out. Alternately, you would be well-suited to any job in which you can function as a loner, working odd hours that you choose, or working at home or away from others as much as possible.

You have a tendency for shyness and self-doubt. This will hold you back until you delve into yourself to find the root cause and work it out. Once you learn to be more extroverted, your life will follow a course of frequent change, new and unexpected opportunities, and spur-of-the-moment adventures. Just when you've adjusted to one set of conditions, you'll move on to another. This is one of the most emotional and dramatic of the Latent Self vibrations, but you need to get out of your own road and not suffocate your own creativity.

13

Under the 13 vibration, you will find opportunities where you can put your practical mind and common sense to good use. You are organized, dependable, hard-working, and dedicated to whatever job you accept. You have a definite sense of right and wrong, which may lead you to consider a career in law enforcement or other first responder roles. Lawyers, judges, prosecutors, accountants, paramedics, and small business owners are often found under this vibration.

At times, you may wonder whether you should set your sights higher and seek a more lucrative career. You may be especially prone to this feeling if your job involves doing the same repetitive tasks every day and you begin to feel like you are stuck in a rut. Instead of contemplating a drastic change in your occupation, explore the opportunities you have in your current position that would allow you to step up to higher levels of responsibility and offer more challenge from day to day.

Under this vibration, you must be particularly careful to avoid lapsing into cynical or judgmental thinking, which could take your thoughts to dark places.

14

As with the 5 vibration, those who are ruled by this Latent Self number are apt to have travel and adventure in their future. You will realize the most success in professions where you are on the go, mingling, socializing, or putting your gregarious personality to work. Careers in the travel and leisure industries, fashion, advertising, photography, theater, dance, music, and professional sports, are favored here. Once you decide on a course of action, you should stick with it and avoid flitting from one job to another merely for the sake of change.

You might not realize that you have a natural flair for salesmanship. It would be advantageous for you to develop the extroverted side of your personality and tap into this attribute. Though you probably aren't drawn to the commercial world, you would do well managing a department store or wholesale warehouse, and in other endeavors where you can put your friendly personality, self-confidence, and power or persuasion to good use.

15

This vibration combines the enthusiasm and inventiveness of the pioneer or initiator (the 1) and the thrill-seeking, gregarious temperament of the adventurer (the 5), built on a foundation of the harmonious attributes associated with the underlying 6 vibration. In one sense, these qualities contradict, and you may find yourself pulled in opposite directions by conflicting interests. You are friendly, open-minded, and diplomatic, and you could find success and fulfillment helping people in the role of a counselor, psychiatrist, occupational therapist, trainer, human resources manager, or similar positions. You are thoughtful and cooperative, loyal, dependable, and empathic. You devote yourself to the needs of those around you. You may tend to stay in a job, relationship, or other life situation for longer than you should and not move on because you feel that others need you, or your current situation is comfortable and secure. Professions in which you interact with children or animals are favored under this vibration. You would also make a good teacher or psychologist, nurse, doctor, or non-profit manager.

16

You are philosophical, thoughtful, somewhat introverted, and quite spiritual. Your emotional life may not be the happiest, which could turn you into a workaholic. You are creative and drawn to the arts. You'll be able to find fulfillment and success in developing your inborn talents for writing, art, music, painting, design, or crafts. On the other hand, you have an analytical streak and a keen intellect which would make you well-suited to scientific research, statistics, conducting marketing research or surveys, accounting, and similar endeavors. Because you invest so much of yourself into your work, you take great pride in your accomplishments, and you are motivated by praise. You will probably work best as a loner or in situations where you have the freedom to set your own schedule and work at your own pace. If you must work with others, avoid being too trusting or mixing your personal problems into work relationships. You may find comfort and reassurance from co-workers or superiors, but it can cause misunderstandings or put you in possibly compromising or embarrassing situations.

17

You are a natural leader, and you have a great deal of ambition and energy, although you are prone to scatter your energy and lose focus. You have many great ideas but may encounter difficulty putting them into motion. Learning to focus on the task or goal at hand will help you consolidate your thoughts and achieve your loftiest ambitions.

This vibration favors business and finance. You would do well in any vocation that involves sales, marketing, banking, investing, or managing resources. Small business owners and self-employed people are often found under this vibration. You are good with money, although you also like to spend it. You are dependable and reliable. You have a knack for seeing problems and coming up with innovative solutions. You are basically honest, hardworking, a good salesman, and a skilled tradesman. You are good with your hands and enjoy building things, whether it's a bookcase, a house, or a profitable business. Learn to keep your ego under control and avoid being overly ambitious or you could alienate business associates and others who can help you reach your goals.

18

You will find your best opportunities for wealth and happiness in professions that allow you to work with people or focus on making your community or the world a better place. Many people who share this vibration are religious; some go into the ministry or pursue caregiving roles as nurses, home health aides, paramedics, doctors, and counselors. Nonprofit organizations could benefit from your caring and insightful approach to solving problems and defining a purpose or mission. You may be tempted to start your own religious, charitable, or educational nonprofit.

Your friends, and even total strangers, often call on you for advice or a helping hand. Sudden, unexpected change is common under this vibration, especially between age 30 to 45. It will behoove you to learn to remain calm and composed under pressure, and avoid the tendency to procrastinate or fall victim to self-doubt and insecurity. You want badly to see the light of higher truth, but sometimes, you stand in your shadow and see nothing. Avoid feeling sorry for yourself when the going gets rough. Work, accomplish, and don't grumble.

19

Under this vibration, life will guide you into situations where you are given responsibility, leadership, and power. You are apt to succeed in whatever you do, but it's not a given because your own actions and attitudes will play a major role in shaping the outcome. You may tend to cut corners or to use "whatever it takes" to reach a goal, which could be your undoing. The 19 is a "karmic vibration," and it signifies misuse of power, either in a past life, say numerologists who believe in reincarnation, or simply a tendency for those fertile conditions to arise in your life and tempt you with tricky choices. Whatever you pursue in work or business (as well as personal relationships), you must exercise fairness, honesty, integrity, and always do the right thing. Be ethical. Avoid any situation that might appear to be a misuse of power, trust, or responsibility given to you.

Life will give you many tests in which you must choose between right and wrong. Making the morally right and ethical choice will bring you success, and the wrong choice will always have painful consequences. It is fairly unusual to have 19 as one's Latent Self vibration, and you can move mountains for the good of all or be at the root of much chaos and despair.

22

You have insight, wisdom, and the potential for greatness. You see exciting possibilities in the mundane and ordinary. You can look at an empty lot and envision a luxury home or magnificent hotel or office complex built on it. You can look at a room and imagine it fully decorated. Or you can meet a person and visualize what he or she would be in their greatest moment of success. This is the vibration of the "master builder," and you can accomplish great things. You enjoy making, building, or designing things. You have leadership ability, and you are dependable, honest, and don't mind working long hours to reach a goal or do a good job. You do not like people who cling to small-minded attitudes, and you often try to help them see the bigger picture. You are positive and optimistic, and your enthusiasm is contagious. You are not especially adept at dealing with people one on one, because you have high expectations and not a lot of patience for mistakes or excuses. You think big, and you want to make a difference in the world. You don't just talk about it—you plan, and you act.

Chapter Four

Determining the Expressive Self

Beyond the Soul Urge, which reflects desires, and the Latent Self, which reveals natural abilities, the third aspect of personality analysis in numerology is the *Expressive Self*. It reveals present conduct—what you are doing in day-to-day living. A closer look at this aspect can yield valuable insights into synergies and conflicts at work in your personality.

To find the Expressive Self, we consider all the letters in the given name at birth—*vowels and consonants*. First, we assign the corresponding number to each letter in the name. Then, we add the numbers for the first, middle, and last name, reducing each to a single digit (1-9). We then add these three sub-totals and reduce to 19 or less, or 22, to discover the Expressive Self vibration.

In this next example, we will continue with the previous name:

```
DANIEL    JOHN    SUTTER
415953    1685    132259
```

Here's the math:

First Name: 27 = 9
Middle Name: 20 = 2
Last Name: 22 = 4
Expressive Self: 9 + 2 + 4 = 15

Here's a quick and easy way to double-check the accuracy of your numerology chart up to this point: Reduce the Soul Urge number (from the vowels in your name) to a single digit (1-9). Do the same for the Latent Self number (from the consonants). Add those two numbers together and the result should equal the Expressive Self number. If your numbers don't add up, you have a math error and must redo the chart. But don't worry. It takes practice to calculate a numerology chart, and much more practice to accurately interpret it.

To interpret the Expressive Self vibrations, consult this table:

Guide to the Expressive Self

1, 10, 19

You are good at coming up with great ideas and devising ingenious plans to develop and promote anything new: inventions, theories, products, start-up companies, social groups. You will find your greatest success running your own business, or as a freelancer where you can work on your own since you find it difficult to confine your thoughts to limits set down by others.

You are determined, courageous, innovative, and you value your independence. You have leadership potential, but people can get on your nerves and you're happier working as a loner. You don't like limitations, and you believe anything is possible if you put enough time and effort into it. You never give up unless there is no other option, and it takes you a long time to get over failure to achieve your goal.

You are outgoing, energetic, usually brimming with optimism and confidence. Sometimes, you can be overconfident and may regret it. You have a great deal of willpower, but you can be stubborn to a fault. You have a vivid imagination and can see exciting possibilities in the most ordinary situations.

2, 11

You are not a leader, and you prefer working alone in subordinate positions. You are an efficient worker, but you don't function well when you are cut off from others. You require human interaction and emotional stimulation.

You are especially good with words, and you can fast-talk yourself and others out of trouble when the need arises. You are tactful, empathic, accommodating, and a good diplomat. You are also a good writer.

You are prompt and courteous, and you expect the same from others. You don't like to be kept waiting, but though it annoys you, you rarely express your irritation because you are averse to causing hurt feelings.

You are artistic, creative, and love color. Many people who have this Expressive Self vibration have a natural flair for drawing, painting, and other art forms. Your imagination makes you an interesting and colorful character, as well as a good story-teller. You are well-liked and respected by many, and you are apt to have a wide circle of friends who enjoy your wit and companionship.

Although you are detail-oriented, you don't enjoy routine or tedious work, and you get bored easily. You need change and variety in your job and your life, or you may move on without warning. You are happiest when you are interacting with people, or helping them in supportive roles, such as that of a counselor, therapist, teacher, or negotiator.

You can be flighty, and you sometimes find it difficult to finish what you've started. A healthy dose of praise or encouragement will usually keep you focused on the task at hand.

3, 12

You are original and creative. Artistic expression is your finest asset, and you could do well in music, art, journalism, dance, or theatre. You should seek jobs and other life conditions where you can put your great creativity and artistic talents to good use.

You are a high-energy person, motivated, confident, and filled with enthusiasm for life. But you grow bored and restless easily. When that happens, you lose focus and scatter your energies. To avoid getting caught in a rut, you may rush projects to completion or leave numerous loose ends, not only in work but other facets of your life. Consequently, some people regard you as flighty, absent-minded, or at worst, fickle and unreliable.

Strive to do your very best, finish what you start, and focus your creative energies on positive goals. Keep your friends close, as you rely on them not only for social interaction but encouragement and ideas. You can be moody, which sometimes puts off people who care for you. Avoid the tendency to become impatient or exasperated with friends who aren't able to keep up with your high energy level or don't always understand you.

Many of the world's greatest writers and artists share a 3 Expressive Self vibration. Its positive and constructive influence can propel you to the pinnacle of success and provide a lifetime of fulfillment. The one requirement is that you must be willing to focus and work hard to achieve success.

4, 13, 22

You are practical, pragmatic, and down-to-earth. You have a firm sense of organization, occasionally to the point of being strict and rigid. You have a natural affinity for business and finance. Architects, executives, chemists, engineers, pharmacists and technicians often share the 4 Expressive Self vibration. Military personnel, pollsters, statisticians, accountants, and administrators are also found under this vibration.

You are detail-oriented as well as mechanically inclined. You have a knack for taking things apart, putting them back together, and making them work. Because you are more focused on the material than emotions, you are usually more adept at repairing objects than relationships. You can be overly practical to the point of seeming aloof or uncaring. You have a stubborn streak, a strong will, and a definite sense of the way things should be.

You are idealistic, principled, and your determination is an asset that will work to your advantage in life. But you can be quite opinionated, which causes friction with friends and family who do not share your views. Strive to be more tolerant and accepting of others who don't agree with you.

5, 14

With the 5 Expressive vibration, you are a "people person," and you gravitate to situations where you can socialize and interact with others. You are persuasive, a good talker, and you are a good closer in sales. You have a knack for making deals. You need a healthy dose of adventure and change in your life. Routine bores you, and when you feel that you might be getting stuck in a rut, you'll rebel and shake things up, sometimes beyond repair, which allows you to move on to new challenges and life experiences.

In your work, you must have intellectual stimulation and variety or you won't stay in a job for long. Because you are so energetic and always looking for the next adventure, your restless nature causes you to move on and sometimes leave important tasks undone. When you are required to concentrate on minute details, your mind is apt to wander, which can lead to careless mistakes.

You are a friendly extrovert and don't often experience bad moods or depression. Others enjoy your company and like being around you. You have a way of energizing a dull party, which works to your advantage, attracting friends, popularity, and more than your share of exciting opportunities in life.

6, 15

Under this Expressive vibration, you have a deep concern for your fellow human beings, especially those who are less fortunate.

Psychologists, counselors, nurses, welfare workers, missionaries, physical therapists, and other caregivers often share this vibration.

It is difficult for you to idly stand by while someone suffers. You are empathic, compassionate, sensitive, devoted, and loyal. Social injustice, racism, and false accusations deeply trouble you. You want to be trusted, and you are quite trustworthy. You don't like idle banter, and you don't like others who gossip. You don't have a lot of patience for the melodramas of other people, although you can get caught up in your own dramas from time to time.

You will be given great responsibilities in life, and you will find success in any endeavor where you are concerned with the welfare of others. There is a tendency under this vibration to experience a variety of health maladies, mostly brought on by poor diet, overwork, and not handling stress well. You concern yourself so much with helping others that you forget about yourself.

7, 16

You are analytical, sensitive, intelligent, and concerned with the ongoing struggles of the world around you. You are fair and tolerant of others, knowing that no one is perfect. Although you don't judge, you can become impatient when friends think and act in ways that don't make sense or seem childish to you.

You would make a good judge or lawyer. You have a deeply ingrained sense of right and wrong. You want the world around you to be stable and harmonious. You are quite curious, and you like to know what makes things tick or why things happen. Detectives are often found under this vibration because of a desire, almost an obsession, to get to the bottom of things.

While you are tolerant of others, you are a perfectionist when it comes to your own actions, and you can be highly critical of yourself. Sometimes, you set yourself up for disappointment by establishing goals or standards that are impossible to achieve. You want to make sure everything is in perfect order before you move on to the next chapter of your life.

You are very sensitive, sometimes overly so, and your feelings are easily hurt by the thoughtless words or actions of others. When you are upset, you will often sulk, go into silent mode, or even fall into the role of a martyr. As a consequence, you may feel unappreciated and misunderstood, which can lead to bouts of depression and, occasionally, self-pity. Avoid the tendency to be disillusioned with friends or loved ones who are caught up in their own lives or dramas and might not immediately realize that you are unhappy.

Your sixth sense is well-developed, and you are very intuitive. You will have many hunches and premonitions throughout life, but you sometimes ignore them and kick yourself for not listening. Pay attention to your inner voice—your hunches are usually right!

8, 17

The 8 Expressive vibration favors success, recognition, affluence, and leadership. You are at home in the world of business and at your best when launching new products or services, starting new companies, coordinating projects, and making money. You can step into leadership roles easily and you quickly earn your colleagues' respect. You also function well in situations where you work alone. You don't like taking orders. If you don't respect a supervisor's abilities, your disdain is readily apparent, which can land you in hot water or the unemployment line.

You are trustworthy, honest, dependable, and you enjoy hard work. You have good judgment and a strong moral compass. You need a great deal of freedom and don't like being tied down or limited. In relationships, you will sour quickly on a partner who tries to control you or box you in. You are attracted to people who are strong-willed and independent like yourself and who can stand on their own. You have zero tolerance for co-dependent relationships, and you'll ghost on a partner who becomes too needy or clingy. You also have little patience for weakness and morally challenged individuals who struggle with addiction or emotional disorders.

You are self-reliant and a natural leader. You inspire the trust and confidence of others, and you work hard to set a good example. When you start something, you always finish it. Sometimes your sense of self-reliance and expecting the same of others can become overbearing. You must avoid falling into the trap of believing that you know everything, or being so overbearing that other people find you egotistical or offensive.

9, 18

You are kind, sympathetic, and understanding. You view the world as one large family. You are trusting, often to the point of being gullible or foolish, and you can be easily led astray. For this reason, you should exercise better judgment in your choice of friends and the people you trust. You always try to see the best in people and expect them to behave in ways that exemplify their better qualities; you are disappointed when they do not.

You are deeply concerned with the welfare of others, and always there when someone you care about needs a helping hand. You may be drawn to professions such as teaching, counseling, medicine, religious activities, psychology, or jobs in the nonprofit sector. You have keen insight into others' problems, and you will work tirelessly to help someone stabilize and move their life on to a positive track.

You give willingly of yourself, but this can leave you feeling drained, and sometimes it allows others to take advantage of you. You are very sensitive, even hypersensitive at times, and your love life is apt to be rather turbulent. Because this is the "finishing vibration" in numerology, you are inclined to see more endings than beginnings in life, which may cause you occasionally to slip into dark moods or depression. Your close friends adore you, but your moods and pessimistic streak can prove difficult for them to handle. Fortunately, your life will be filled with many close friends, and when some of them need a break from your intensity, others will step forward to encourage and cheer you on.

Chapter Five

Determining the Life Path

*E*veryone travels on a certain road through life. At each turn, we meet with a new set of conditions, new opportunities and obstacles, new aspirations and dreams, new pitfalls that can trip us up. As we go through our day-to-day existence, we grow, hopefully; we gain new knowledge, useful insights into ourselves, and a better understanding of the world around us. In numerology, this road that we travel from birth until our final day in this material world is called the "Life Path."

Some numerologists accept the theory of reincarnation as a given and base chart interpretations and readings on this premise. They believe that before birth, the soul chooses the experiences that it will undergo in this lifetime. The soul is indelibly imprinted with a knowledge of past and future and knows what life lessons it must undergo to evolve to a higher level of spiritual development, the eventual goal of which is perfection and harmony with the universe. Thus, what we experience throughout life, for better and worse, is not by mere coincidence.

This belief that we follow a life path that stretches from birth to death should not be taken to mean that events and situations are pre-ordained and therefore unavoidable—numerology teaches that every human being has freedom of choice in every matter. Nothing in life is set in stone—you can turn left or right on your life path. You can turn around and backtrack to a previous point. You can stay in a particular set of conditions for an entire lifetime, or move on at any point. Freedom of choice is always the cardinal rule in life. But as we travel this path, we encounter signposts along the way. We experience swift currents that carry us forward, and headwinds that hold us back. These ever-changing influences can be anticipated and accurately identified through numerological analysis of the Life Path vibration and related aspects in a chart.

To determine your Life Path vibration, add the numbers of your date of birth. Treat the month, day, and year as three subtotals as you did previously with the first, middle, and last name. Reduce all three to single digits, add them together, and then reduce as needed, following the rule explained below.

To determine a person's Life Path, you must know the correct day, month, and year of their birth. Use the calendar month value —January is 1, February is 2, March is 3, and so forth.

This example will walk you through the Life Path calculation:

```
June 26, 1985
Month:  6
Day:    2 + 6 = 8
Year:   1 + 9 + 8 + 5 = 23 | 2 + 3 = 5
```

Add these three values together:

```
6 + 8 + 5 = 19
```

For the Life Path, we apply a special rule for arriving at the reduced total: reduce it to a single digit (1 – 9) or any of the five karmic vibrations: 11, 14, 16, 19, and 22. Because the sum of the example above is 19, we do not reduce it further. The Life Path vibration for this birthdate is 19.

Numerological interpretation of the Life Path can be complicated as it requires taking other aspects of the chart into account. The resulting insights can provide a remarkable glimpse into what lies ahead on one's path through life. Being that this book is meant to be a basic introduction, the table below provides a brief and rather simplified overview of the Life Path interpretations.

Guide to the Life Paths

1

Your life will be positive and constructive. You will find yourself in situations where it will be necessary to learn the lesson of individuality and stand on your own. You admire courage and independent thinking in others and must cultivate these attributes in your own life, if you have not already done so. You will be entrusted with positions of leadership and must learn to use your authority for positive and constructive ends. Most important, you must avoid setting in motion the cause-and-effect consequences of misusing your authority or power for selfish or destructive ends.

This Life Path brings frequent change and unexpected opportunities. Sometimes, change will occur with breakneck speed, and you'll marvel at the surprising opportunities that fall into your lap.

2

On the 2 Life Path, you will find yourself placed in frequent situations where your ability to remain calm and stable will be tested. You will find yourself scattering your energy and must focus on staying organized and devoting your attention to the challenge or task at hand. This is a positive, harmonious vibration that portends a pleasant, happy life.

Friends will be important to you, and you'll make new friends easily. You must guard against repeating the same mistakes and the tendency to fall into ruts. Impulsive decisions can bring disappointment and heartache under this vibration, so learn to think things through and avoid hasty decisions or acting out in a moment of drama or intense emotions. Close friends and family will play an essential role in your life, rescuing you more than a few times from difficulties of your own making.

3

Under this vibration, life will be an adventure with rarely a dull moment. The 3 Life Path favors material comfort and affluence, with a strong focus on creative self-expression. You may yearn for peace and quiet, or the serenity of a happy home; but you won't have much time to be a homebody, and you will have more than your share of travel. Sudden changes are in the cards, especially before age 32, followed by an extended period of stability from the late 30s into the late 40s.

Romance will be exceptionally important to you, and it is very likely that your partner will play a crucial role not only in your emotional happiness but also in your professional success. This vibration favors mixing business and romance, and spouses often are business partners too. Common scenarios under this vibration would include a writer, artist, or actor paired with a publicist; healthcare professionals or caregivers working together in one practice, or partners who co-found an entrepreneurial endeavor.

You will have many opportunities to profit from the mistakes of others if you keep your eyes open and pay attention, as you are a fast learner. This will help you avoid setbacks and failure. Try not to act out and make impulsive changes without much thought when you find yourself stuck in a period of boredom or repetition. Most of the unhappiness that you will experience in life will be of your own making, and when you learn to restrain your impulsiveness and inclination to become involved in pointless drama, you will be able to reach the pinnacle of success and happiness.

4

On the 4 Life Path, your life will be productive and stable. You will work hard, which you will enjoy, but occasionally you will gripe that you must work harder than other people to get ahead. The good news is that your efforts and dedication will pay off, attracting success and prosperity into your life. Material comfort and affluence are favored on this Life Path.

You will find your greatest opportunities mingling with people who share your views and who are from your own walk of life, which allows you to meet them on common ground. You must learn to be more tolerant and compassionate towards others. There is a tendency under the Life Path to lose friends because you can be set in your ways, opinionated, and judgmental, which could also cost you opportunities in career and business endeavors.

You are dependable, trustworthy, and good with money—your own and that of others. You are organized, detail-oriented, and a great researcher. You will do well in any work where you can put those talents to use, such as in engineering, accounting, machinery design or repair, technology, or science. Lawyers and judges often have a 4 Life Path, as do law-enforcement personnel, financial advisors, stock brokers, mid-level executives, and administrators. Much success and happiness will come to you as long as you cultivate open-mindedness and don't become so entrenched in your ways that others find you impossible to get along with.

5

Under the 5 vibration, your life will be a fast-paced, nonstop adventure. You will find yourself in situations where a gregarious, extroverted personality will open doors to wonderful opportunities. Your life will be buffeted by unexpected change more often than you might like. Also, being constantly on the go can have an adverse effect on your health. Being accident-prone is not unusual under this vibration. You must therefore avoid pushing yourself to the brink of exhaustion, maintain a healthy lifestyle, and avoid risky and dangerous activities as much as possible.

Many people who share this Life Path are strongly drawn to physical sensation and gratification. There is a risk of addiction to cigarettes, alcohol, sex, or drugs under this sensation-seeking vibration. It is especially important for you to protect your physical and emotional health by avoiding such behaviors and embracing holistic life choices.

You tend to scatter your thoughts and energies, leaving unfinished tasks and loose ends that later come back to bite you. Learn to channel your energy into the goals that you most want to achieve, and finish what you start, even if you realize midstream that it won't bring the results you'd hoped. You will be the captain of your ship, and ultimately, you will decide by your actions the level of success and happiness that shines into your life. Keep your eye on the ball and succeed, or squander your efforts and let wonderful opportunities slip through your fingers.

This Life Path highlights travel, socializing, and mingling with important people. You will attract more than your share of opportunities because of your magnetic, upbeat personality. But your desire for quick results with minimum effort can lead to difficulty. Be on guard against shady dealings and get-rich-quick schemes that may cost you more than you would ever stand to gain.

You will often become immersed in the problems of family and friends. At times, you are irresistibly drawn into their dramas like a moth to a flame, but you always manage to extricate yourself. You may find it hard to remain in one place for very long because you yearn for constant change, variety, a wide circle of colorful friends, travel, and above all, adventure.

6

Marriage, family, home life, caring for others, and compassion are strongly highlighted on the 6 Life Path. A surprising number of people who share this vibration will find true love and long, happy marriages; childhood sweethearts are also favored. But this Life Path can be challenging for others. They yearn for intimacy yet avoid or fear it, and then complain that it is not attainable. Some of these individuals will experience a string of failed relationships until they realize that partners whom they are pursuing are incompatible. Often, there is also a tendency to go for looks rather than substance. When they tweak their wish list and preferences, they will greatly improve their prospects for making the right connections and forging deep, lasting relationships.

If this is your Life Path, you are compassionate, romantic, and affectionate, a natural empath. However, your empathy can cause you much suffering, as you are prone to trust the wrong people or invest your energy into people who are unwilling to change. You are constantly giving of yourself, but in the process, you do not pay adequate attention to your own health and well-being.

Your friends see you as a starry-eyed romantic, and sometimes you are exactly that. You can be impulsive at times, but your common sense will usually keep you out of difficult situations. You can be careless with your words, and it won't take long in life for you to realize that blurting out your feelings is rarely a good idea.

You are loyal and faithful, and you would sacrifice your own goals, even martyr yourself, for those whom you love. You are very sensitive, and your feelings are easily hurt. You are prone to depression when life doesn't go the way you hope. The 6 vibration will put you in many situations where you must use your common sense to make wise choices, and mistakes will have painful consequences. You sometimes find yourself wondering why other people can seemingly skate through life with ease and never pay for mistakes while yours have dire consequences.

You are not always emotionally stable, and you tend to get lost in the maze of details in day-to-day living. You try hard to focus your attention on your goals, but you sometimes lose track of what you set out to do and end up going around in confused circles. Life will lurch forward in fits and starts, with periods of unforeseen change, even chaos, followed by weeks, months, or several years of relative calm. As long as you avoid impulsive behavior and follow the dictates of your common sense, your life will be happy, and you will love deeply and be loved.

7

Deep emotion and spirituality are highlighted on this Life Path. It is not always an easy vibration to live under because emotions and spirituality often are at odds. You are not the most stable person, and your feelings can carry you from one drama or crisis to another until you learn to stabilize and get your emotions under control. You have a natural curiosity and are drawn to unusual people and situations like a moth to flame. You must learn about life in all its stages and strive to acquire as much knowledge and understanding of human nature as you can.

You tend to be quiet and introspective, and you have probably experienced more than your share of disappointment and heartache. You are wise and caring, and you have deep insights into other people; but you often misjudge the people you trust and their intentions, which can lead to unfortunate consequences.

You have an inquiring mind and are analytical, but you also have a secretive side and an impulsive streak. At times, friends don't understand you and may wonder if you have a split personality. You are constantly looking for insights into yourself and why you think or feel a certain way. This can lead your friends to think you are self-absorbed or even selfishly preoccupied with your own feelings. You may devote a lot of time to yearning for happiness but may come away thinking that you might never find it.

On this Life Path, you are capable of success, but you are not driven to accumulate wealth or become famous. You are more interested in gaining respect and achieving financial security for the comforts and peace of mind it provides. Many natives of the 7 vibration have spurts of chaos and high drama in their lives, but most of the time it is of their own making. Your friends are colorful characters, offbeat, creative, and sometimes full-on weird.

8

This Life Path accentuates success, wealth, power, and leadership. You will be placed in situations throughout life where you are called upon to take charge and lead. Many who share this vibration are somewhat introverted, and might even be shy or reserved; but these qualities will not take them very far toward their goals, and they will find success by developing their leadership potential and the personality traits that empower a strong leader.

Great financial success and recognition are likely on the 8 Life Path. However, you can be your own worst enemy, and you must guard against flashes of temper, or conversely, feelings of inadequacy. Otherwise, precious opportunities will be lost.

Life will move along for you with great leaps and bounds, and then you will lapse into a period of stability and hard work to lay the groundwork for your goals and accomplishments. At times, this will leave you feeling that you are stuck in a rut. Realize that any major goal worth achieving takes an investment of time, and you must patiently work through the steps to reach the end result. As long as you remain focused and maintain a positive, optimistic outlook, every goal you dream of will be within your reach.

9

Those who share the 9 Life Path can look forward to reasonably happy lives. In numerology, 9 is the "finishing vibration," and you will spend more time and energy than most people on dealing with unfinished business, tying off loose ends, and going back over the details of your endeavors and tweaking the details. You will be drawn to offbeat jobs or unusual professions.

You are very sensitive, and you enjoy recognition for your efforts, but you are not so concerned with what others think of you. Sometimes this apparent disregard for the feelings or opinions of friends and colleagues will make them feel put off. This could hinder you by creating emotional headwinds or hard feelings that you will need to work through.

You are an individual in every sense of the word, but your life belongs to the world. No matter what time of the day or night, your friends and even acquaintances will seek out your advice or a helping hand. Although it can be draining, you rarely object and are always eager to help. Given that this scenario will likely prevail through much of your life, if you pursue an occupation that focuses on helping others, such as a counselor, minister, doctor, or other caregiving or support roles, you can build a career and earn a living doing what you would be doing anyway.

11

Life will put you in situations where you must relate mundane daily experiences to the spiritual or universal level, and to karma. You may be preoccupied with higher truths and the actions you must take to attain inner growth or accomplish your goals, but family and friends will often dismiss you as cool and aloof. Because of what's going on in your thoughts and your life, you may come across as disinterested or unfeeling to the people you care about, but you are merely engrossed in problem-solving. You are an enigma, and you can be difficult to know or understand. However, under your cool exterior, you are deeply concerned with the state of the world, and you have a heart of gold.

The 11 Life Path is often associated with psychic influences and metaphysics. You'll have strong hunches and premonitions, and experience will teach you to listen to your inner voice. You can sometimes intuitively predict what is about to happen in your life to the astonishment of your friends. Occasionally, your prescience is so startling that it spooks even you. Some people on the 11 Life Path have uncanny dreams that come to pass. Instead of being apprehensive about this natural ability, learn to accept it as a sixth sense, a natural extension of your five normal senses, and it will provide invaluable insights in your life.

You are capable of great success, and it's possible you may achieve world-renown. You can drive your goals forward on an accelerated trajectory using your keen intellect and your uncanny understanding of human nature. You easily win support for your ideas and plans; but be careful to choose your projects wisely. Not all of your ideas are practical or worth the effort, and if you rally support for too many ideas that lead nowhere, those around you may think next time, "Oh no! Not another crazy scheme!"

Everything you do is powered by fierce willpower, tireless effort, and keeping the end result in your sights as you move forward on a project. You can be a compulsive workaholic, and you have a visionary streak. You sometimes limit your success or effectiveness by insisting on doing everything yourself. This arises from a deep-rooted belief that no one can do the task as well as you can. Learn to delegate—in fact, it's quite possible that someone else can do the task as well or even better than you can! When you involve others in your projects, they become more committed, and the end result often will be better than you ever thought possible.

You refuse to accept that anything in your life is beyond your control. You believe that you have full control over your thoughts, your feelings, and your destiny. You can become impatient and frustrated when something does not go according to plan, and you can become angry when a metaphorical wrench is dropped into the machinery. Learn to avoid striking out at others and blurting out your frustration when you encounter setbacks or delays, or you will lose friends and supporters that you will later regret.

14

The influences and trends at work on this Life Path generally are the same as for the reduced 5 vibration. However, this is a karmic vibration, so it has special meaning. It enhances or intensifies some of the effects associated with the primary vibration.

Your life will be an "always on the go" adventure, but too much of a good thing can be detrimental to your physical and emotional health. You may find that trying to keep up with the fast pace of your life is stressful and exhausting, and your friends and family may not be able to keep up at all. Over time, this can take a toll on you, so you must focus on maintaining a healthy lifestyle. Take up meditation, yoga, or other techniques to help you relax, balance, and manage stress.

You will often find yourself in situations where a gregarious personality will open the door to opportunities for success. But sudden, unexpected change also will be a factor in your life, and it will occur more frequently than you'd like. Clinging to physical sensation and addictive behaviors is fairly common in people who share this Life Path, and they may have difficulty with overeating, drinking, smoking, sex, or drugs. Strict adherence to moderation and a healthy, balanced lifestyle is important. A tendency for being accident-prone is also typical of the 14 vibration, so dangerous occupations and sports should be avoided.

You tend to scatter your thoughts, take shortcuts, and leave things undone which later come back to bite you. You should learn to direct your energy into the goals you most want to achieve and finish what you start. Ultimately, you alone will decide the level of success and happiness that you bring into your life. You can either keep your eye on the ball and succeed, or waste energy and let opportunities slip through your fingers.

This Life Path highlights travel, socializing, glamor, luxury, and mingling with movers and shakers. You should learn to be more discriminating in your choice of friends and avoid dubious business deals proposed by shady characters who do not have your best interests at heart.

16

The 16 vibration has many of the qualities that one would find on the 7 Life Path. However, it is a karmic vibration and thus has special significance, intensifying some of the effects associated with the reduced primary vibration. For instance, the 7 is very emotional and prone to impulsiveness; these qualities are more pronounced under the 16.

Because it is associated with hypersensitivity, inner conflict, and mood swings, the 16 can be a difficult vibration in daily existence. It promotes instability, insecurity, and lack of confidence, which can manifest in various ways, particularly, jealousy and possessiveness. Those who share this Life Path may jump from one drama or crisis in life to another until they eventually learn to stabilize and get their emotions under control. Absent that, some of these unhappy souls will probably end up in co-dependent or abusive relationships.

While the effects of this vibration are more pronounced and it has more downside than the 7, we must remember that numerology does not predict what will happen, but only shows the trends and vibrations in effect and what is apt to happen if a person does not assert free will. At any time, we can take steps to avert a vibration's negative pitfalls and accentuate its positive qualities.

You are very inquisitive and are drawn to unusual people and situations. You are quiet, introspective, perhaps shy, and you love being in love—it is essential in your life. But you are a dreamer and an idealist—you demand the perfect love, which does not exist, so you inevitably walk away disappointed and go on to the next.

You are wise and caring, and you have deep insights into other people. But you are prone to misjudge those who are close to you. You are not a good judge of character; consequently, unscrupulous and dishonest people find it easy to deceive you or take advantage of you. Life will put you in situations where you will be required to exercise better judgment and be more selective in your choice of friends and lovers. Eventually, you will learn this lesson and your emotional affairs will take a turn for the better.

You are constantly looking for insights into yourself and why you think or feel as you do. This can lead your family and friends to think you are too wrapped up in your own feelings. You devote considerable effort to your search for happiness, but you often take a glum view and worry that you will never be happy.

You will be given opportunities for success on this Life path, but you are not driven to accumulate wealth or to pursue great fame. You are more interested in gaining respect and financial security for the sake of your comfort and peace of mind it provides.

19

The 19 has many of the qualities that one would find on the 1 Life Path. However, being a karmic vibration, it has special meaning. It intensifies certain effects associated with the underlying 1 vibration. Its main challenge, and the potential downfall of those who share the 19 Life Path, is the karmic consequence of a misuse of power, as we discussed in an earlier chapter on the Soul Urge. In fact, the appearance of this vibration in the Soul Urge and the Life Path is interpreted in much the same way.

To recap what we covered earlier, numerologists who accept the theory of reincarnation view 19 as an indicator of a karmic debt from the past that must now be settled. Something was taken from the universe that was not paid for, and the debt is now due and payable. Others view it as a "misuse of power," perhaps earlier in one's life, or it could represent a situation in the future where that temptation may arise. A third school of thought is that the 19 is an unwieldy mix of fresh beginnings (the 1) and resolute endings (the 9), which creates a contradiction. Some interpret it as the phoenix rising from the ashes, or new forest growth in the aftermath of a fiery holocaust that destroys the forest yet restarts the cycle of life anew.

Life may be challenging under this vibration. It brings sudden change, sporadic progress, and unexpected delays. Plans surge forward and stall just as suddenly. Some goals are achieved with almost no effort; others seem forever elusive, and one may be tempted to give up and pursue a different course.

You will be given choices throughout life that require great thought and discernment. It is critically important that you make the right choice and avoid any hint of a situation in which power or authority at your disposal could be misused—shady business dealings, fraudulent transactions, falsified credits on a resume, and so on, all must be avoided. For the most part, the negative aspects of this vibration can be avoided by making wise choices and pursuing constructive actions throughout life.

22

On this Life Path, governed by the "Master Vibration," you will be given many opportunities to achieve success, wealth, power, and spiritual enlightenment, or to at least work toward that lofty goal. You must recognize your inborn abilities and develop a plan of action for putting your best characteristics to constructive use. You are highly intelligent, motivated, resourceful, and down-to-earth. The sky is the limit for you, as long as you do not stand in the way of your own progress. This Life Path will require you to be organized, dependable, and practical in all of your undertakings to accomplish your goals. If you express the negative qualities associated with this vibration (demanding, judgmental, narrow-minded, unrealistic expectations), much stress will bubble up in your work and relationships, and you'll hinder your own progress.

On the 22 Life Path, you'll find yourself in situations where others depend on you as a steady, sensible, down-to-earth force, and a pillar of strength. You'll be called upon to be the Master Builder and to move projects forward and achieve results.

This is a favorable Life Path that portends a productive and successful life. You'll be given leadership roles where you must use your common sense and pragmatism. You'll be given opportunities to teach and help others develop their abilities. Many natives who travel this Life Path will build great and memorable things. Avoid rigid idealism and narrow-mindedness or you may pay a steep price for your inflexibility. Also, remember that while you don't often make mistakes, when you do, they are apt to be very large ones; so, you should be particularly diligent about investing the extra time and effort to ensure that you don't make them at all.

Chapter Six
Determining the Karmic Essence

Another crucial element in a numerology chart is the *Karmic Essence*. In previous chapters, we learned about the three vibrations that influence personality: Soul Urge (desires), Latent Self (abilities), and Expressive Self (present conduct). We also examined the Life Path, a distillation of influences that one can expect to encounter throughout life.

Sometimes, these vibrations are compatible; other times, they don't fully sync, or they may even conflict. For example, let's assume that we have a numerology chart for a woman named Kanesha, who has a 6 Soul Urge and a 6 Latent Self. These two aspects are complementary and suggest that she will be motivated by a desire for romantic fulfillment and a happy home. The 6 Latent Self reveals that she has an innate ability to form deep, lasting relationships and to build a close-knit family and stable home life. In other words, she has the ability to achieve her heart's desires.

But what if Kanesha has an 8 Expressive Self and 16 on her Life Path? Now, the waters are muddied, and her chart reveals conflicting influences. The 8 indicates that she will be focused on material goals and the pursuit of success, leadership, and power. Romance and home life will take a back seat to career and business interests, either by choice or necessity. Likewise, the 16 Soul Urge is not especially favorable to happiness in love. So, as she goes through life, not only will her attention be drawn away from her desires, but the influences on her Life Path will move her even further away from those desires.

How do we make sense of this complex jumble of vibrations? We need a window into the big picture—some indication of how it all comes together to create the whole person whose chart we are interpreting. We can get that big picture, or a strong hint of it, from the Karmic Essence vibration. It combines the Soul Urge, Latent Self, Expressive Self, and Life Path to reveal a more in-depth profile of an individual's personality, behavior, and future trends—in other words, it reflects the essence of who that person is.

To determine the Karmic Essence, reduce the Expressive Self and Life Path values to a single digit (1-9). Then, add the two resulting numbers together, as shown in this example:

```
Expressive:    17 (1 + 7) = 8

Life Path:     16 (1 + 6) = 7

Karmic Essence: 8 + 7 = 15
```

To reduce the Karmic Essence, follow the rule given earlier for the three personality aspects (Soul Urge, Latent Self, and Expressive Self) and preserve the secondary vibration. Reduce the sum to 19 or less, or 22. Thus, in the above example, we see that the Karmic Essence vibration is 15.

Consult this table to interpret the Karmic Essence vibrations.

Guide to the Karmic Essence Vibrations

1

You are strong-willed and independent. You have a deeply ingrained sense of right and wrong, and it is difficult to lead you astray. You enjoy the spotlight and when you are in a group, you are usually one of the most outspoken people in the room. You can liven up a dull party, and friends enjoy hanging out with you.

You are ambitious, energetic, and a natural leader. You will have many opportunities in life to build constructive things of a lasting nature, but you must avoid the pitfalls of this vibration, which include: scattering your energy, wasting time, cutting corners to hasten progress, and taking unnecessary risks. You have tremendous potential for success, and most of the setbacks you encounter in life will come from your own carelessness or inclination to rush things.

In love and marriage, you prefer being the dominant partner, and you take the lead whenever you can. You like having the final say, so it would be prudent to find a mate who is content with being the passive half of your relationship and letting you have your way. You have a strong ego and sense of pride, and when things do not go your way, you can react with moodiness or flashes of temper. If this behavior is not checked, it will lead to tension in your romantic relationships, lost friends, and disgruntled coworkers.

You could benefit from learning to better understand and respect the feelings of others. You can be rude and offensive, and you will pay a high price for this behavior in life.

You love deeply and are fiercely defensive of your family and friends. Often, however, you don't show your deeper feelings, and loved ones may have a sense that you take them for granted.

In business, you find it difficult to work under superiors. You are always inventing new gimmicks and seeking to improve on the old ways of doing things. You should be at the head of your own company or self-employed. However, if you strike out on your own, you should be prepared for some hard lessons brought on by your stubborn disposition and insistence on having your way and the final word. Life will show you that you have much to learn, and the sooner you begin to rely on others who have more knowledge or experience than you, the better.

Among friends, you set the trends and establish the fads. Your views and opinions are respected by all. Friends often ask for your advice on important decisions or help with problems. You enjoy this because it makes you feel recognized, useful, and respected.

Most of the time, you find it practically impossible to spend a quiet, relaxing day at home. You are full of energy and must always be on the go, working or doing something that you consider worthwhile. Channel your energies constructively and you will achieve great success, affluence, and recognition.

2

You are compassionate, open-minded, empathic, and unpretentious. You are always willing to lend a helping hand, even when you are in the midst of your own problems. You are very sensitive. You prefer cooperation and harmony and prefer to avoid confrontation whenever possible. You tend to be soft-spoken and easy-going. Because you are so caring and kindhearted, people often try to take advantage of you, and when you discover that someone has betrayed you, it hurts deeply, although you rarely mention it. You should learn to be more assertive in your day-to-day relationships, and not put up with being taken for granted or abused.

You are kind and gentle, and you can be loyal and trusting to a fault. You want to see the best in everyone. In love, you are open, honest, and you do not enjoy emotional games. You are not flirtatious or promiscuous, and you intensely dislike people who are. You often call people out on behavior that you don't like, and you especially abhor two-faced people and hypocrites.

You tend to be a martyr across the whole spectrum of your relationships, and you can resort to passive-aggressive behavior when you are hurt or upset. It is best for you to avoid falling into this state of mind since it can cause major friction, and more often than not, the people close to you don't realize that you are upset—you just come off as pouting or brooding.

You need a down-to-earth, honest, and dependable mate that you can look up to and respect. You would get along with a strong-willed partner because you have a cooperative and sunny disposition. You don't often insist on having your own way, although on matters that you consider quite important, you will draw the line and your demands are nonnegotiable. Avoid involvements with partners who are passive or have a personality similar to yours, as there would be no one to lead or make decisions. The resulting relationship would be wishy-washy and mutually unappealing.

In friendship and family matters, you would rather follow than lead, but you enjoy planning events and working with others to accomplish worthwhile goals. You are not particularly ambitious, and you have no desire to be the life of the party or set the agenda. You prefer doting on your friends and family and devoting yourself to brightening the daily lives of everyone around you.

You are a good listener, and people appreciate you taking an interest in their well-being. You are popular and rarely make enemies. You are tactful, optimistic, and diplomatic. There's no argument or rift so serious that you cannot quickly make amends and set the relationship right.

In business, you have no burning desire for wealth, fame, or fortune. You appreciate creature comforts and financial security, but you are not particularly ambitious or driven to pursue material goals. You shy away from positions of authority. You prefer to work with people one-on-one, listening to their problems, offering advice, and helping them find solutions to vexing issues in their lives. For this reason, you would be well-suited to occupations such as counselor, therapist, psychologist, minister, negotiator, social worker, or any work where you can use your people skills and infuse others with your optimism and cheerful disposition.

You will probably find it advisable to avoid positions of leadership and authority, and avoid executive roles in your own business. You do not have the drive, ambition, or hard-nosed management skills necessary to build a major company and keep it running profitably. Many individuals who share this vibration feel bad about mailing out invoices for services rendered and charging for their time. You must learn that your time is valuable. People often associate the value of a service with how much you charge, and they see freebies and steeply discounted services as inferior or worthless. Most of all, you must learn to put your foot down and not allow people to take advantage of your kind disposition and generosity.

3

You have many talents, and you are driven to express yourself through art, writing, music, or other creative venues. You are imaginative, very intelligent, and capable of inspired ideas. You have keen powers of observation and a vivid imagination. You can see deeper meanings in the trivialities of day-to-day existence. You should learn to harness this hyper-awareness and use it to enhance your creativity.

You are gregarious, enthusiastic, and make friends wherever you go. You surround yourself with colorful, interesting, artistic people. Others may think that some of your friends are weird, but you enjoy seeing the world through their eyes and hearing about their unusual life experiences.

Although you may seem confident and self-assured to others, your self-esteem is low, and you sometimes doubt your own good looks and abilities. You worry that others will see your flaws as major faults that outshine your virtues. As a result, you may seem self-deprecating and insecure. Sometimes you become so inwardly focused on what's wrong with you that friends see you as detached, self-absorbed, or depressed. You won't fully realize your full potential for success and happiness until you dust off your mirror and discover your true worth and appeal. You have something worthwhile to offer the world, and you have the power to bring light into the hearts and minds of everyone around you.

In love, you tend to be flirtatious and secretive. You are constantly in search of perfect love, but you are swayed by physical beauty and sex appeal. A partner whom you consider alluring is not necessarily one you'll want to marry and spend your life with.

You worry too much, and your nerves are constantly on edge because you are high-strung. Sometimes you exhaust yourself from stress, which adversely affects your health. You can have drastic mood swings, which creates a roller coaster ride for friends around you.

Once you form an emotional attachment, you have high standards and expect your partner to live up to them. You have an eager, adventurous approach to life, and you are fun to be with. This isn't necessarily a positive when it comes to building a committed relationship, and you may find it difficult remaining loyal to one person. Avoid the tendency for thrill-seeking or you may spend a lot of time alone and lonely.

Because natives with this Karmic Essence lack confidence, they tend to be insecure, which can lead to fits of jealousy and possessiveness. Because you look for partners who are self-reliant and like freedom, these clingy emotions don't go over well and you may cause more than a few relationships to crash and burn. Above all, you should find a partner who is tolerant, patient, devoted to you, and who can handle your moods.

In friendship, it takes time for you to warm up, but when you finally let down your guard and display your likable, high-energy personality, you make friends easily and they enjoy your company. You sometimes get caught up in drama and may turn one friend against another through idle gossip

You may struggle in business and career matters because you scatter your energies, lose focus, and flit from one thing to another without finishing what you start. Sometimes you come across as aloof or preoccupied because your mind is on more important things than your job. This may become a source of trouble for you throughout life until you learn to focus and apply yourself diligently to the task at hand.

You will likely follow a creative path in life, and you will pursue it with your eyes open to the fact that it might not be financially rewarding, but it is a creative choice that you believe you must make. You will do well in whatever you attempt, and you are capable of producing wonderful artistic works if you apply yourself and keep your emotions firmly rooted on stable ground.

4

You are organized, sensible, detail-oriented, and pragmatic. You are firmly grounded and rarely indulge in daydreams or let your mind wander. You are a hard worker, dependable, and loyal. You are an effective leader when placed in positions of authority, but you take charge only when necessary and don't actively seek out those roles. You could achieve considerable success and wealth, but you are more interested in concrete results and accomplishments than power. Once you settle into a job or profession that suits you, it will become the most important focus in your life. You enjoy work and often take your job home so that you can keep working afterhours. If you are not careful, you could become a workaholic, which will take a toll on your social life and love life.

Loyalty is one of your greatest virtues. You never turn your back on friends in need, and you will help them out of any problem, no matter how great. You are honest to a fault, and you expect honesty from the people around you. You can be brutally honest, even when no one has asked for your opinion, which can lead to hurt feelings and broken friendships. Taken too far, you can be rigid, judgmental, and narrow-minded, which can work against you in every department of life. You may need to learn to be more tolerant and open-minded or you will end up with only a few friends, and they will all think like you do.

Most natives of this Karmic Essence are conservative, some are deeply religious, and they have a strong sense of morality. They know right from wrong, and they avoid people and situations that do not fit their world view. Leave your mind open to new ideas, and you'll gain deeper insight into life, and more friends too.

In the business world, you can make it to the top, but you will likely stop before you get there. You are not driven to be number one, the best. You would be just as happy as number two or three, and being the absolute best that you can. It's likely you would be content with the job of assistant director, or a department head rather than the CEO. You aren't terribly interested in expending the time or energy required to inspire and lead other people.

This Karmic Essence favors a comfortable life, enough financial security to get by without struggling, a spacious home, a couple of cars in the driveway, and a couple of kids who grow up and go on to college, all made possible by your hard work, of which you will be very proud.

You are detail-oriented and have a high degree of manual dexterity. You are good at taking things apart, effecting repairs, and putting them back together again. Thus, you would make a good repairman. Many of these natives are highly skilled tradespeople and are found working as carpenters, electricians, plumbers, and in other building trades. This Karmic Essence likewise favors any profession in which attention to detail is important, including: lawyers, architects, doctors, police, fire fighters, and paramedics; also, accountants, stock brokers, and bankers.

In romance and marriage, you are honest, loyal, and rock-solid dependable. You won't ever stray from your partner or be unfaithful, and you expect the same in return. You love deeply and respect your partner just as deeply. Domestic life in your home is likely to be stable and peaceful, but you need to choose a partner wisely, because some may find your temperament and lifestyle rigid, tedious, or boring. Choose your mate from the Earth vibrations (see Chapter 11) for a relationship that will be long-lasting, harmonious, and mutually fulfilling.

5

Under this Karmic Essence, you will strive to maintain your freedom and independence, even if it means breaking off a relationship that has become too limiting. Natives of this vibration resist being tied down or loaded with responsibilities. They dislike routine and seek constant change. Thus, they are on an eternal search for something new, different, and original.

You enjoy change for the sake of change. Your life will be prone to sudden change, and you may move around often, change jobs, and jump from one romance to another, often without warning. You'll likely get a thrill out of taking risks, and you may consider a dangerous occupation for the sheer thrill of it.

Your health is vulnerable under this vibration, and you should strive to maintain a wholesome diet and lifestyle. Because this vibration accentuates physical sensation, you are more apt to be a smoker, drinker, or to seek out pleasure from sex and recreational drugs. Consequently, one downside of the 5 vibration is a risk of abuse or addiction to sensory stimuli. There is also a tendency for accident-proneness. This is all the more reason to maintain a healthy lifestyle. Avoid over-indulgence and self-neglect.

These natives are fun-loving, popular, and have many friends who share the same temperament of always looking for adventure and a good time. You can get along with practically anyone, but most of your friendships are superficial and brief. You may have a few close friends over the course of your life, but most are merely fellow revelers and passing acquaintances.

Travel is accentuated under the 5 Karmic Essence. It's likely that you will see more than your share of travel, and much of it will involve extended trips far from your home base. You may have a yearning to see the world, mingle with many different kinds of people, and explore the many levels and conditions of life.

This vibration does not especially favor love and marriage, in large part because it is so focused on constant change, adventure, and being on the go. Thus, it is possible that you will not find much happiness of a lasting nature, unless you change your priorities and aggressively pursue it. You will be prone to flit from one relationship to the next, enjoying one-night stands and moving on to the next. You don't embrace responsibility, and the idea of settling down in a long-term marriage interests you about as much as a bowl of prunes. You want to live for the moment, one day at a time, enjoying life experiences as they arise, and then passing quickly on to new places, new friends, and a new tomorrow.

In business and finance, you will likely achieve mid-level success and recognition, although your inclination to move from place to place and job to job will probably hinder your prospects for advancement. You would do well starting your own business, which would give you the freedom to set your own schedule, pursue financial opportunities where the wind blows you, and invest as much or as little energy into your enterprise as you wish. The downside of this vibration is that if you approach your business in a lackadaisical way or you do not shoulder the responsibility required to keep it running, your success will be very limited, or your venture will falter.

You are a good salesman, and you can be quite charming and persuasive. You also would be a good con man; but you must avoid unscrupulous behavior and unethical schemes under this vibration or it will lead to self-inflicted misery and failure. Also, guard against extravagance and waste.

6

You are kind, sympathetic, understanding, and you have a great deal of empathy, which causes you to experience the feelings of others on a very personal and sometimes disturbing level. You are a good listener, a good friend to those in need, and a good counselor. You have a deep understanding of human nature, and you are patient. You never expect more from people than they are capable of. You are overly trusting, and you can be easily misled. You are generous to a fault, which can cause considerable grief because you find it very difficult to say no to anything, regardless of the sacrifice required of you.

You are warm and extroverted, and you make friends easily. You view your friendships as precious, and when you form an attachment, you expect to know that friend for many years.

Others often perceive you as quiet, shy, and passive, without a lot of backbone. Although you may present this façade, in fact, you are strong-willed, tenacious, even stubborn, and you resolutely pursue what you want—which more often than not involves love, home, family, and material comforts. You are not necessarily ambitious, but you are determined: you know what you want in life, and you will invest the time and energy to achieve your goals.

In business and finance, this Karmic Essence favors a reasonable measure of success and financial security, but it does not usually portend leadership or power. You are not motivated by a desire to get rich or build empires, and you do not want power over other people's lives. You may marry into money or come into an inheritance; otherwise, you'll focus on earning enough to get by and finding a job that you enjoy. You probably lack good business sense and won't do well at investing. When you spend too much time focusing on money, you can become anxious or frustrated, so you would rather just keep the whole subject in the back of your mind or not think about it at all. Don't allow friends to talk you into risky schemes, or you'll end up losing your money and friends. You are too trusting and prone to fall for a sad story, which could leave your savings depleted.

You can fulfill your fondest hopes in love and marriage, as this vibration favors romance and a happy home life. Most of the people who share this vibration yearn for the simple pleasures of a loving family, a couple of good kids, and a comfortable home. You would find your greatest happiness spending the day with your partner, strolling on the beach, or standing on a mountaintop overlooking a pine forest or the city lights below.

Your best prospects for a happy marriage will be with a strong, dependable, loyal mate who enjoys physical affection and who will reciprocate your loyalty and devotion. Ideally, your partner will agree to take on the responsibility for paying the monthly bills and making key decisions so that you can enjoy your life free of stress.

A partner with a strong 8 influence in their chart, or a 4, would be well-suited to you. Avoid those governed by 5 (thrill-seekers) and 7 (too moody and analytical). A partner with a strong 1 or 3 influence might make for a lasting relationship, but they may be too erratic and off in the clouds for your taste.

7

You have a great deal of wisdom, but not many people realize how deep you really are. You sometimes wrap yourself in a protective cocoon because you are very sensitive and hide your emotions for fear of being hurt. You are quiet, at times shy, and introspective on the surface; but deep down, you are seething with emotions. You throw cold water on love, yet it is essential to your happiness.

You are spiritual, and you have a highly developed sixth sense. You will have many hunches and premonitions throughout life. Some who share this Karmic Essence have prophetic dreams. They are highly empathic and often know what a friend or loved one is thinking or feeling, although they may keep these insights to themselves.

You have an analytical mind. You are practical and down to earth most of the time, as long as your emotions aren't too involved. When a problem arises in daily life, you study it from every possible angle. When you are ready to act, you know just how to handle the situation.

You are continually trying to understand your purpose in life and your place in the world. You have a deep desire for inner peace and tranquility. You have a lot of faith in human beings, though you don't always believe they deserve it. People can win your trust easily, but those who take you for granted soon realize that you are always observing and evaluating whether they are worthy of your love and support. You can turn off and distance yourself in an instant when you lose faith in someone.

You will have a few close friends in life and many acquaintances. People often come to you seeking advice for their problems.

Even complete strangers seek you out. Sometimes this amazes you, because you have days when you can barely decide how to handle your own issues. As you enter your 30s, this steady wave of needy people will annoy you, and you may resent that so many depend on you. But even as you yearn for tranquility and solitude, you are never stingy with your time or advice, and you are always on call for your family and friends.

In the business world, you can achieve success and prosperity, but you may find it necessary to detach from your spiritual views, or they may interfere with your ability to pursue financial goals or compete for advancement. You should invest a great deal of time and thought into choosing a profession because once you settle on a career, you will regard it as a lifelong choice, even if you are unhappy in that job or occupation.

You are an advanced soul, and you have a deep understanding of human behavior, karma, and universal laws. You are intelligent and spiritually aware, and you have much to give of yourself to friends, family, and others around you. Individuals who share this vibration often include scientists who make world-changing discoveries, lawyers, judges, and those in professions that involve analysis, research, mathematics, and other sciences. However, dark moods and depression can stop some of these individuals in their tracks. They need to learn inner balance and better ways to manage their deep feelings and emotional mood swings.

In love and marriage, you may not be easy to live with. Many who share this vibration blow through several marriages before they connect with the right partner. You highly value intimacy, and you are capable of deep, passionate love. But you are apt to wander and may have numerous affairs that leave you feeling guilty. You may be romantically or physically attracted to lovers who are far older or younger than yourself. Your ideal mate should be relaxed, easygoing, stable, not prone to intense moods, practical enough to keep you balanced, and grounded enough to handle your moods. They should also be strong-willed and dominant enough to keep you from running off the tracks when you decide to test your boundaries or when life throws you a disappointment that you have trouble handling.

8

Leadership, wealth, and power are accentuated for those who share the 8 Karmic Essence. You will be given many opportunities in life, and you'll be able to go as far as your ambitions will carry you. You are strong-willed, intelligent, courageous, dependable, and confident. You have leadership skills, and you can assess a situation and immediately know what needs to be done to fix a problem or achieve success.

You don't shy away from hard work, and you pursue goals with tireless determination, optimistic that you will quickly reach the end result. When you want something, you set your sights on it, shift into overdrive, and never give up.

Practical and pragmatic, you are a resourceful problem-solver. Your feet are planted firmly on the ground, and you have little patience for wishy-washy people, daydreamers, or complainers. You can be a workaholic, and you expect those around you to work just as hard. You have a great deal of physical stamina. If you decide to invest the effort, you will succeed at everything you do.

Despite your incredible drive and intense focus, you can be moody, temperamental, easily frustrated at times, and you have a temper that comes out when people don't carry their weight or live up to your high expectations. You also have a stubborn streak, which is an asset until you find yourself obstinately pursuing a goal or outcome that isn't worth your time or simply won't turn out.

You have many friends, but not many are close, and you trust even fewer. You tend to keep people at arm's length, and you try to avoid deep emotional attachment, both to friends and lovers. At times, you are cynical, and you may revert to believing that people around you want something from you or have other motives.

You project yourself as a pillar of strength endowed with an unwavering sense of purpose, but you are not always self-assured.

Occasionally, you have flashes of self-doubt, and you worry too much about failure. When you get into this state of mind, you may procrastinate on something at great length as a way to avoid making decisions or acting when you are unsure of the outcome.

In business and finance, you will not find it easy to take orders and work under superiors. You should start your own business or manage a company for someone else. You work best when you are calling the shots, planning, carrying out decisions, and directing the flow of activity. You handle responsibility well. You can be trusted with secrets, and you will never betray a confidence.

You love a good challenge, can't handle boredom, and you'll quickly lose interest in routine or tedious jobs and move on. You will find your best stride when you are planning or launching major new undertakings. Whatever you touch will become profitable. Once you have money, you are thrifty and quite capable of managing your finances.

In friendship, you are outgoing, outspoken, and always up for a party or social gathering. You can be flashy, even flamboyant, and you like others to see you as a trendsetter. You are opinionated and can be narrow-minded, but you don't go out of your way to provoke arguments or force your views on others. When people disagree with you, you'll usually argue up to a point, then drop it and write them off as uninformed or not worth your time.

You are protective of the people you care about and generous, but not to a fault. You will usually help a friend in need, as long as you feel that he is making a real effort to help himself.

You go out of your way to avoid people who engage in petty gossip, as well as lazy people and liars. You have a deep sense of morality and avoid associating with people who don't live up to your high standards. You are always candid with your friends, and you expect the same from them. You intensely dislike bullies, mean-spirited people, and hypocrites.

You are a fan of leaving work at the office, and you know how to have a good time. You may not be the life of the party, but people enjoy hanging out with you. You have a great sense of humor when you are comfortable with the people around you.

You enjoy stimulating debates, but sometimes lose your temper when proven wrong, and you may lose friends as a result. You give the impression that others must take or leave you, and you're comfortable in your own skin. But you have a weak spot that few are aware of—you worry about what others really think of you or what they say about you when you are not around.

Under the 8 Karmic Essence, your love life is apt to be erratic and prone to sudden changes. You want a home and family, but you may see it as being more of a status symbol than fulfilling a need for deep intimacy. Some natives of this Karmic Essence treat their close friends better than romantic partners, whom they sometimes take for granted or neglect because they are more focused on material goals. You enjoy intimacy and physical affection, but it is not essential. You can take love or leave it, although it's nice to have a home to return to after work.

You have high standards for a partner in love or marriage, in part because you consider yourself quite a catch. You expect a lot, but you don't always reciprocate. You may have a string of illicit affairs throughout life, but you don't usually develop emotional attachments to any of these flings. You may approach affairs as oddly therapeutic—a chance to let off steam, enjoy spending time with someone new, and then you are ready to move on.

Ideally, your mate should be at least somewhat ambitious and willing to work with you as well as socialize with you in business circles. You might even prefer a marriage of convenience that provides the benefits of a home and loving partner, and the freedom to roam with no pressure over long hours at the office or not being around for a child's violin rehearsal on open house night. You do have the capacity for lasting love, and if your partner plays their cards right, you may settle into a long-term, faithful relationship.

9

The quest for emotional fulfillment and happiness is never far from your thoughts. You crave security, a happy home, and roots. But life will give you frequent reminders that you belong to no one person but the world, and you cannot be tied down.

You are philosophical, open-minded, and deeply religious or spiritual. You are flexible and can adjust to any condition or circumstance that life throws your way. From time to time, however, you will resist change and cling to the familiar comforts around you. After much reflection, you'll make the difficult choices that you must make to fulfill your greater purpose in life.

Under this Karmic Essence, you will have many friends, and you will put considerable effort into trying to maintain deep and meaningful relationships with them all. You are honest and loyal for the most part, and you do not like liars, hypocrites, hurtful gossip, or two-faced people. When you find such a person in your circle of friends, you will usually turn against them, cut them off, or treat them rudely until they get the message and go away. Despite your effort to maintain deep friendships, they don't usually last very long, and you reluctantly let go, moving on to different friends. You do make a serious effort to keep in touch with old friends by phone or mail.

In business, you are better suited to working under superiors than trying to establish and lead your own business or organization. You probably lack the hard-nosed qualities necessary to start and grow a profitable business, although you probably do well in a nonprofit environment.

In love and marriage, you will gravitate toward prospective mates who are sympathetic, thoughtful, gentle but strong, generous, and concerned about the problems and injustices in the world today. In any relationship, you will thrive only if you are allowed total freedom of thought and action. If your partner tries to own you or hold you back, your romantic attraction and affection will fade, and you will drift away.

The 9 Karmic Essence can be challenging for those who are intent on finding happiness in love or enjoying a happy family and a home with a white picket fence. All things in life are possible, because we have free choice in our lives, but 9 has a reputation as the finishing vibration, and it can be stressful on love and marriage. Separations often occur, although the love may remain intact.

10

(See Number One)

11

If this is your Karmic Essence, you are spiritual, intuitive, sensitive, and emotional. You are an inspired daydreamer who believes that if a person can dream it, they can achieve it. You have a well-developed sixth sense, and you'll have many psychic experiences, hunches, and even prophetic dreams throughout life.

You are original, inventive, bold, and daring. Fascinated by the past as well as the future, you will likely spend quite a bit of time daydreaming about both. You also tend to cling to the past, even if it is littered with unhappy memories, because it is familiar and comfortable, and it keeps you from having to move forward into the vast unknown of the future.

You are deeply concerned with the conditions that affect mankind and the world. You see things on a philosophical and universal level. Global issues such as climate change, racial injustice, war, and poverty deeply concern you.

You have seemingly unlimited energy, enthusiasm, and drive which often amazes the people around you. You are hard-working, but tend to work in energized spurts. You put everything you have into causes that you believe in and into helping family and friends in need. Sometimes, you will do the same for a complete stranger.

Despite your deep understanding of human nature and the universe, you can be stubbornly narrow-minded. You often see things as black and white, and when you form an opinion or world view, you're willing to walk through fire for your conviction. This can leave your friends with hurt feelings, and your obstinance may drive some away. You usually regret your stubborn streak, and if you care enough about a friend, you'll apologize eventually.

Throughout life, you will become involved with a wide variety of movements and causes aimed at social reform or making the world a better place. You are a firm believer in the teaching that every human being in this life should leave the world a better place than it was when they came into it. You have a basic love for nature, humanity, the ocean, and starry night skies. It all takes on a magical quality for you and fills you with awe and wonder.

You often become so engrossed in theories and principles that you come across as preoccupied or absentminded to friends and family. At times, you can become so enthusiastic about your beliefs that you seem fanatical, which may cause some consternation. You love teaching, and you have a natural talent for it. You are very intelligent, and you enjoy sharing your knowledge and experiences with others. You like knowing that you have helped other people grow and discover new directions in life. It doesn't matter what you are teaching, the experience is gratifying, and your students are awestruck by your wealth of knowledge and the patience you have in sharing it.

You could be a charismatic leader, but you must learn to be more receptive to new ideas and change. You think of yourself as progressive, and many of your ideas are inspired or even revolutionary, but you cling to old-fashioned attitudes and beliefs. You may lay down the law on how to live your life and expect others to follow your lead and embrace your views. You need to recognize that not everyone has the strong devotion and fire of higher wisdom burning in them, and not everyone is as concerned with spiritual awakening as you are.

Always be ready to cheerfully embrace the error of your ways when it is pointed out to you, and be willing to change course and embark on a new direction when it's appropriate. Remember that the world's greatest leaders and teachers never stop growing and learning. No living human being has all the answers.

In business and finance, you may achieve some success and affluence if you do not obsess over it and struggle after it. Guard against unscrupulous business practices at all times. Some people who share this Karmic Essence believe that the means justify the end, and this can lead to unfortunate endings. Ultimately, you are a creature of the spiritual world, and while material comforts are nice to have and you might desire them, you will probably make choices that stress other priorities.

In your social circle, you are quite popular and many friends think you are wonderful—but people either love you or hate you, and you have antagonists who intensely dislike you or think you are full of beans. Your almost evangelical zeal to share insights into life as you see it can turn people off. You can convince many people of the veracity of the most ridiculous idea—but not everyone!

The friends who stick around in your life—and there will be many—have great respect for your intellect, insight, and courage. They would do almost anything for you, and that is because you would do almost anything for them. You are generous and give of yourself freely. In fact, you are the type of person who would skimp on your own dinner to help a hungry friend. Many of your friends think you are fascinating, perhaps weird, but fun to hang out with and always a source of good conversation about anything and everything under the sun.

In romance and marriage, you probably won't be content with a mate who professes ordinary love for you. Your partner must live up to the laws that you follow, and must have the same depth and passion in their soul. You may tend to be impatient with your mate, and if they do not grow quickly enough, you could become disillusioned and go cold on the relationship without warning. As a consequence, you may have a string of affairs in which you seek the qualities you desire from others. How you handle the temptation to wander will determine the longevity of your relationships. Ultimately, you are searching for the perfect match—your soul mate, an intellectual and spiritual partner.

All things considered you are not easy to live with. You can have mood swings and your emotions can be erratic. You understand universal concepts but don't do as well at understanding your partner's feelings and needs. If you want to have any chance at a long-term, gratifying relationship, look for a partner who is sensitive, gentle, spiritually aware, understanding, and most of all, very patient.

12

You will be challenged throughout life to merge the diverse qualities of the numbers making up this Karmic Essence—the bold originality and independence of the 1, the mild, cooperative disposition of the 2, and the creativity and artistic expression of the underlying 3 vibration. If these influences are positively aligned in your chart, your challenge will be to tie loose ends together in ways that will move your life and goals forward. If negatively aligned, you must cultivate and learn to apply all three influences: stand on your own feet, be independent, strive for a cooperative, balanced demeanor, and express yourself through whatever artistic talents you possess. In any case, you'll need to stay focused and avoid getting stuck in ruts or resisting change when familiar conditions are more comfortable. If you let your creative talents blossom, they will carry you to great success.

You are imaginative and highly intelligent, but you sometimes doubt your abilities and stand in your own way. Some individuals who share this Karmic Essence have deep-rooted feelings of insecurity or an inferiority complex. You should work on developing self-confidence and believe in your true worth. Realize that you have something wonderful to offer the world, and let your creative feelings and vision bubble to the surface.

In friendships, you are popular and outgoing. Being a high-energy person, you are always up for a good time. You enjoy gossip a bit too much and may lose friends over careless words or by taking sides when in situations where you should remain neutral.

Keep your best friends close, as you rely on them not only for social interaction but moral support and ideas. You can be moody, which can put off those who care about you. Avoid becoming impatient or exasperated with friends who cannot keep up with your high energy level or who don't always understand you.

In the business world, you will probably change jobs often. A variety of jobs will interest you, but none will hold your attention for very long. Your restless spirit will drive you to the next set of new conditions. You have almost inexhaustible energy but you become bored easily. When that happens, your thoughts wander and you scatter your energies. You may rush projects through to completion and leave many loose ends, not only in work but in other areas of your life. People often regard you as flighty and fickle; at worst, some may see you as irresponsible.

Those who share this Karmic Essence may delay career decisions until relatively late in life. They can achieve success and affluence in whatever profession they pursue, but in many cases, their prospects are limited because they are not willing to settle down and do the hard work necessary to reach worthwhile goals.

Successful writers, artists, and actors share this vibration. It is an inspired, constructive influence that can propel you to success and recognition, as long as you focus and are willing to work for it.

In intimate relationships, you are not an easy person to live with. You need a partner who is patient and understanding. You require a lot of attention and encouragement, but sometimes you get so caught up in your own feelings or problems that you don't reciprocate, causing your partner to feel neglected or hurt by your apparent disinterest. You can go hot and cold in a relationship without warning, which can impact your long-term outlook for happiness. Cultivate stability, make a special effort to reach out and let your partner know that you care, and strive to keep your emotions in check in day-to-day existence.

13

This vibration exemplifies the daring individuality of the 1, and the creativity and artistic temperament of the 3, built on a foundation of organization and practicality from the 4 vibration. These influences should work to your advantage, opening the door to prosperity, friends, and a life of adventure—or many difficulties that arise from being pulled in opposite directions. Fortunately, you know how to channel your energies efficiently, and when you set your mind on a goal, you will work tirelessly to achieve it.

You yearn for change and new experiences, and you dread the prospect of boredom or being stuck in a rut. Despite this, you often resist change, even when you believe it is in your best interest. Thus, you may end up stuck in a rut, the very situation you fear. In spite of your cool and self-assured demeanor, you can be insecure and unsure of your abilities. You crave recognition and work hard to achieve it. Workaholics are often found under this vibration.

You are not always discreet, and until you make a conscious effort to cultivate a faithful temperament, your love relationships will probably be fiery and short-lived. You sometimes become involved in your friends' dramas, which are none of your business and will cause you to expend much energy unnecessarily.

You can be a person of many contradictions. Love is important to you, but you are not particularly comfortable with intimacy, and you don't like to get too close. You yearn for adventure and change, yet you can be set in your ways.

You consider yourself progressive, and you are generally openminded. But you have an almost superstitious fear of the unknown and the future, and some of your friends regard you as narrow-minded. You have a deep sense of right and wrong, but you don't always practice what you preach. You can be judgmental and at times view the world in black and white. You must remember that others won't always agree with you, and they are entitled to their own opinions.

In friendship and romance, you place a high value on loyalty. You are fair and strive to be honest. You are rarely flirtatious. But you have a jealous streak and can be possessive. You have a temper that sometimes flares when your heart is involved, and you should learn to control the impulse to lash out with harsh words that you may later regret.

In career and business, you should look for opportunities to put your practical mind and common sense to good use. You are organized, dependable, hard-working, and dedicated to whatever job you accept. Your firm sense of right and wrong may spark your interest in a career in law enforcement or other first responder roles. Lawyers, judges, prosecutors, accountants, and paramedics are often found under this vibration.

At times, you may wonder whether you should set your sights higher and seek a more lucrative career. You may especially feel this way if your job entails doing repetitive tasks every day and you begin to feel like you are stuck in a rut. Instead of contemplating a drastic change in your occupation, explore opportunities in your current position that would allow you to step up to higher levels of responsibility and offer you more challenge from day to day.

You must avoid falling into cynical or judgmental thinking, or narrow-mindedness, which may take your thoughts to dark places.

14

Complex and conflicting influences are at work under this Karmic Essence. Because 14 is a "karmic challenge" vibration, it can have far-reaching effects on one's life, creating unique challenges and pitfalls. When negatively expressed, many who share this vibration will cling to physical sensation and self-destructive behaviors such as addiction, risk-taking, and accident-proneness. This is the flip side of the high-energy and adventure-loving 5 vibration. As always, they have free will and can choose whether to express the vibration's positive attributes or allow the negative qualities to express in daily living.

The 14 Karmic Essence blends the originality and individuality of the 1 vibration with the practical, organized and detail-oriented sensibility of the 4. The two vibrations are not especially compatible, and it becomes even more complicated when you factor in the underlying 5, which is outgoing, adventurous, and carefree. This may cause you to feel pulled in conflicting directions throughout life.

You truly enjoy being a free spirit and cherish your independence and individuality. You try to infuse a touch of the unique in all that you do. At the same time, a part of you wants to keep your feet planted on the ground and prefers to be a detached recluse. You want to work things through methodically and focus on details. How you merge these contrasts together in daily living will determine whether the life story you write will be a wonderful success or a frustrating ordeal in which you continually trip over loose ends, procrastinate, and cannot decide whether to rush forward or plod along methodically.

You may find it difficult to profit from past mistakes, which will cause you to repeat the same lessons. Two lessons you should strive to learn early on: avoid taking shortcuts that rarely turn out, and avoid jumping to hasty conclusions and rash decisions. You must balance the urge to leap forward impulsively with the opposing desire for caution and steady progress. Your life will then take a positive turn, and your prospects for success and happiness under this vibration will multiply.

You must pay close attention to your health, both physical and mental. Many people who share this vibration have an addictive personality and habitually overindulge. Proper diet, sleep, exercise, stress management, avoidance of addiction, and minimizing risk-taking are prudent choices.

You have a strong curiosity about life and want to try everything at least once. You love having a good time, and your friends enjoy your company. You are gregarious and love going to new places and trying new things. You have a knack for helping friends climb out of a funk, and you encourage them by pointing out the silver lining in every cloud. At times, you speak before you think and must remember that your careless words can offend others without you realizing it.

In career and business, you can achieve great success, but be careful about the tactics you employ. You are clever, adaptable, and progressive, but you also can be scheming and may stray into dishonesty, extravagance, and vice. Some people under this vibration will acquire great wealth only to squander it and die broke.

In friendships, you are popular and the life of the party. You make friends easily and enjoy hanging out with creative, offbeat, eccentric friends. Avoid the habit of using people and discarding them as you move on to new life experiences.

In romance, you enjoy the search for love and starting a new relationship more than the hard work of maintaining or deepening an existing relationship. You tend to lose interest quickly and move on to the next affair. You may confuse love and sex, which can lead to misunderstandings with partners and broken relationships. You are not likely to remain faithful for very long, and your eye and heart may stray. Yet, you expect your mate to be devoted and faithful. You need to realize that one-sided romances of this sort rarely work out. Your best chance for happiness will be with a mate who also has a 14 Karmic Essence or a similar vibration that accentuates creativity, individuality, and personal freedom.

15

This vibration combines the bold individuality and inventiveness of the pioneer (1) with the gregarious risk-taking qualities of the adventurer (5), built on a foundation that favors stability, harmony, and romantic bliss (6, the reduced vibration). These influences do not mesh well and may cause friction in love relationships as you swing back and forth between passive and aggressive; brash and mellow; adventurer and homebody. Likewise, you may be indecisive or conflicted in your life ambitions. It will take serious effort to get these competing tendencies in sync and make them work to your advantage, but it can be done, especially if you use your ingenuity and problem-solving skills to think outside the box. You might, for example, start a business that offers caregiving services, a marriage planning firm, or a family counseling practice, which are favored under this Karmic Essence. This would allow you to draw from the diverse pool of your talents and natural inclinations.

You are friendly, compassionate, dependable, and diplomatic. You are loyal to a fault and always consider the needs and feelings of others. You have strong empathy, which can be a blessing and a curse: sensing the thoughts and feelings of others can be insightful but disturbing too, causing you to feel sorry or guilty for how others feel.

In friendships, you are extroverted and make friends easily. You will have a wide circle of friends, and some of your friendships will last a lifetime. People enjoy being with you, and you have a good sense of humor. Unfortunately, you have a tendency to trust everyone, and this can lead to problems and disappointment.

You cling to old friends, even after they're gone from your life. You are reluctant to toss their phone numbers, just in case you may need to get in touch again. It would be good medicine for your soul to do an annual housecleaning and unload those bits of paper. Let go of the past and lighten your load so you can move forward with enthusiasm into the future.

In career and business, in addition to the suggestions given above, you could find success in any job or profession where you are helping people one-on-one, such as a counselor, psychiatrist, nurse, or teacher (especially teaching young children). Your love for animals could lead you to become a veterinarian. You would also be well-suited for any job in the nonprofit sector.

You will tend to remain in a job, relationship, or other life situation for longer than you should. You may hesitate to move on because you are comfortable and secure in your current situation. Your desire for roots and security (from the 6) is stronger than the adventurous, secondary influences (from the 1 and 5). You should learn to emphasize the latter so that you do not waste time and energy on life situations that you know you should change.

In romantic relationships, you yearn for the simple pleasures of a happy marriage and a comfortable home life. Love is essential to your soul, and without it, you are miserable. You will make a good partner in marriage because you are affectionate, cooperative, and willing to meet your mate more than halfway to keep the peace in your home.

You will likely fall in and out of love often. You seek the perfect soul mate who warms your soul, and when you realize that a partner doesn't quite fill the bill, you move on to the next. You have a bad habit of getting ensnared in your friends' dramas. You should gossip less and worry more about your own situation.

You are one of the easiest vibrations to live with. Although you can be jealous and possessive, you realize it stems from your insecurity, and you usually can deal with it. If your partner does something to offend you, you won't hesitate to bring it up, but you are always tactful.

You love music. It's likely that you have musical talents, and you may play an instrument. You have a great sense of rhythm, and you are probably a good dancer. You have an affinity for nature in all its beauty. Long walks on the beach, in the mountains, or on local hiking trails will help you stabilize and rejuvenate when needed. An afternoon in a beautiful natural setting will help put you in the mood to make important decisions.

Because you are so sensitive and giving, the people you care about sometimes take you for granted. Do not allow yourself to be trapped in abusive relationships. Be more cautious in your choice of friends and lovers—trust only those who earn it.

You can become overwrought about matters of little consequence, and you spend far too much time worrying about things you have no control over. It would be helpful to your state of mind if you kept a copy of the serenity prayer on your desk and referred to it when you are feeling highly stressed:

"God, grant me the serenity
To accept the things I cannot change,
Courage to change the things that I can,
And the wisdom to know the difference."

Shortcomings of the 15 Karmic Essence include jealousy and possessiveness. You are highly sensitive and moody, even on your good days. You invest much of yourself into your relationships because you fear losing the one you love or being abandoned. This makes you susceptible to bouts of anxiety and depression. The sooner you learn coping mechanisms for dealing with these feelings, the happier you will be. Also, don't let others dump guilt trips on you. It's easy to make you feel guilty; manipulative people know this and will use it against you. A good rule of thumb in daily living is: when you a have good reason to feel guilty, own it and apologize. When you have no reason...do not feel guilty!

16

With the 16 Karmic Essence, complex and conflicting riptides of mostly emotional nature are a force that requires careful interpretation. First, we must realize that this number is a "karmic challenge" vibration, which means that it will influence a person throughout life, both in subtle ways and sometimes very dramatically, presenting distinct pitfalls and challenges.

In its negative aspect, the 16 warns of "emotional crucifixion," which in numerology means that there is likely to be a marked tendency for broken relationships and emotional upset as a consequence of actions in a past life. As with all karmic challenge vibrations, something was taken from the universe or thrown out of kilter that must be put right. This does not mean that natives of this vibration are doomed to turmoil in love or a string of divorces. But it does reflect a tendency for this to happen, if you do nothing to change the landscape and alter the day-to-day vibrations and influences in your life. So, one can freely choose wisdom (which is the positive manifestation of the 7 vibration) over chaos and emotional strife. In fact, these natives are capable of finding the purest and greatest form of happiness because of the spiritual balance brought about by the constructive application of wisdom and the other positive attributes of both the secondary vibration (1 and 6), and the primary vibration (7).

After considering its role as a challenge vibration, we consider the secondary elements: we see the originality and independence of the 1, and the sensitivity, compassion, empathy, and domesticity of the 6. This actually works to the advantage of those who share this Karmic Essence, making deep, passionate love attainable. On the other hand, if an individual resorts to the negative and destructive behaviors associated with this vibration through deception, infidelity, vindictiveness, abuse, and similar actions, the consequences will be painful, because karma—the law of cause and effect—is in play. You inherit the wisdom and judgment from the 7, and you are expected to use it. You should know better than to plant seeds of chaos and turmoil; if you do so anyway, then it is reasonable to expect that you will reap what you sow.

As for your personality under this Karmic Essence, you are highly sensitive, intelligent, and spiritual. You have deep, intense, and at times stormy emotions; but you usually maintain a calm façade and few people realize how emotional you really are. You have an analytical mind, but despite that, you are not particularly stable. You can drift into dark moods and depression without warning. You have wisdom far beyond that of most people, and your challenge is to learn to use it to improve your own life and benefit those around you.

You are reserved, introspective, sometimes shy, and often give the appearance of being distant, aloof, or detached. You have a keen mind and submit all problems to thoughtful analysis, dissecting and examining a problem until you arrive at a logical conclusion.

You have more than a passing interest in spiritual matters. You may practice meditation or other spiritual exercises, and you are very psychic. You will have uncannily accurate hunches and premonitions throughout life, and they happen so commonly that you take them for granted.

In spite of your outward calm and collected appearance and your logical reasoning abilities, beneath the surface you are a bundle of nervous energy and conflicting emotions. Many times, you will spend long hours delving into a problem. You will arrive at a logical solution, then ignore it altogether and act with incredible impulsiveness. You know the difference between right and wrong, but your intense emotional drive makes it difficult for you to follow your conscience.

In friendships, you gravitate toward people who have much in common with you—people who are forever struggling to achieve inner peace and emotional bliss. You are not particularly loyal to any group of friends, and you vacillate from group to group. You don't like being tied down in one place and burdened with responsibilities.

In business and finance, you will probably attain some wealth and public recognition, but you quickly scatter your funds. Money seems to slip through your fingers and your extravagant nature makes thriftiness difficult. You would do well in any profession where you have some degree of independence. Working with material and employing your fine sense of observation, such as in a laboratory, would be most rewarding. You can tolerate minute detail and you are highly adaptable.

In love and marriage, you are searching for the perfect mate. You know exactly what kind of relationship you want. However, because you are so idealistic, your love life may be disappointing.

You are promiscuous and loyalty is one of your weak points. You insist upon maintaining a high degree of freedom and independence. Finding the right mate will probably be difficult since you have such high standards and you rarely. stick with one person for very long. You are constantly looking for the perfect form of love, or at least an example of it, and although you realize you have set your goals too high, you never compromise „or lower them.

The 16 vibration symbolizes divorce, affairs, and emotional crucifixion. People who are governed by this essence seem to have grave emotional difficulties, and many of them simply shy away from love, concentrating on the career aspects of life instead. In spite of the apparent faults and shortcomings of the 16, this vibration is the most emotional and sensitive. The person born under the 16 has a perfect understanding of people and emotions. The 16's difficulty, however, stems from a combination of karmic debt—the need to make up for past violations of the laws—and the failure to apply accumulated knowledge to themselves. The 16 must learn to practice what it preaches.

17

The 17 vibration combines the originality and ingenuity of the 1with the spirituality and analytical qualities of the 7, melded together with the overarching influence of the 8 vibration. This can bring opportunities throughout life to assert bold leadership in daring new directions, or your pride and unwillingness to admit you are wrong at times could lead you and your followers into delusional pursuits or off a cliff. Life will imbue you with material success and wealth, but you must guard against overworking yourself, as well as a propensity for overexuberant pride and vanity. Protect your health from too much stress and anxiety.

You want recognition and find it difficult to work unless someone is nearby, constantly boosting your ego. You have excellent control over your emotions as a general rule and you never mope over failures or mistakes in marriage. You simply try again, but you'll try another approach.

You are well-organized and a good manager You are usually

dependable, but you can be quite careless and irresponsible when you want. You are moody and changeable. You accomplish only when you feel like working.

You are a strong leader, but you should avoid impracticalities and daydreams, for they are your pitfall. You are not too concerned with how a particular feat is accomplished, so long as it gets done. The means you use in achieving your desires are not important. It's the end that counts.

In friendships, you are the leader of the group, and you are always around to help others out of their troubles. You may become involved in several minor violations of the law simply to see if you can outsmart society. You tend to be rather rebellious and in your younger years, you often shock people by your dress or behavior to get attention. You are always interested in social movements. Some of the great reform leaders were born under this vibration. You are also spiritual and intuitive, a power for good.

In business and finance, you can go far and attain a high degree of success if you could only concentrate on one thing at a time. Unfortunately, your thoughts seem rather scattered, and you may be tempted to switch from one money-making scheme to the next without accomplishing anything.

You are often drawn to get-rich-quick schemes, but rather than adding to your financial status, you usually lose when the entire project backfires.

In friendship, you are strictly loyal. Once you make a friend of someone, the relationship is long-lasting. The people with whom you associate are colorful and eccentric, but as far as you are concerned, they can do no wrong. You would go to any length to extricate a friend from trouble. But you may not have many friends because you strike others as arrogant and superior. It is not easy to get close to you.

In love and marriage, you will make a fine mate, but your moodiness and constant desire for change and activity can make you somewhat difficult to live with. You should choose a mate from one of the Fire vibrations for the best relationship. You must retain your freedom of thought, however, and not be tied down or loaded with responsibilities.

You are fairly loyal so long as your home life remains cheerful. If the going gets rough, however, you may justify infidelity as being necessary to your well-being.

18

You are emotional and long for the glamour and excitement of romance. You are not too discreet and some of your views on life are highly unrealistic. You should retain a down-to-earth outlook. Stop being so aloof and withdrawn and you will find an immediate improvement in your disposition. You seem constantly tense and irritable, and this is because you are prone to be apprehensive about the future. Relax and live one day at a time.

In business and finance, you can achieve a moderate degree of success if you force yourself to follow practical guidelines and stop wasting energy. You are strong on systematic organization, and you have deep insight into human nature.

Your friends are mostly warm and decent individuals and you are proud of them. You are an excellent judge of character so long as your emotions are not too involved. Friendships with you are meaningful and long-lasting. You want all relationships to be "give and take" affairs where mutual trust and understanding are of the utmost importance.

In love and marriage, you will probably suffer several major disappointments because your attentions are scattered and you have a difficult time remaining with any one person. You are interested in everybody and there have been times when you have felt closer to a complete stranger. You may be involved with occasional secret romantic affairs, but this is necessary for your growth and independence of thought.

19

The 19 essence can be a difficult vibration. It indicates a former misuse of power; a karmic debt that resulted must now be paid.

You will find yourself placed in positions of leadership but forced into difficult decisions throughout life. You will look to others for advice, but only you will have the knowledge of which way you should turn. You will be given a clear choice between what is right and wrong, and the decision you must make will often be on the spur of the moment. You will turn to friends and relatives for answers and assistance, but you'll discover they are of no help at all to you. You must dig into yourself to find the answers.

In the financial world, you are liable to attain great success, but you must guard against employing negative energies to satisfy your ambitions. You have a good sense of firm leadership, and you are original and creative. You can work well with people because you have a perfect understanding of the human mind. You can go all the way to the top, or you can sink and fail miserably. For you, there is rarely a halfway point.

In friendships, you are fickle and cautious. It is difficult for you to get close to other people, because no relationship can exist unless you think it will be meaningful and worthwhile. Your standards are high and you will have many acquaintances who consider themselves your friends, but few true friends who you accept. Once you do become attached, however, you are loyal and devoted for life.

In love and marriage, you are easily swayed. Prospective romantic partners who present themselves with an air of mystery can intrigue you and lead you astray. You crave love and emotional security, but you may often get sex and love confused.

You are not an easy person to live with. You have sudden mood changes, bursts of energy in fits, and by your compelling desire to change the world into a better place. You are forever spreading truths and voicing opinions on the way you see things. You should learn to pay more attention to the feelings of loved ones.

22

You are idealistic and highly intelligent. You are occasionally reckless and you will experience many sudden changes in life. You are good at organization and can dominate any situation or circumstance if you apply yourself. The 22 essence is powerful; it is called the "master number." It brings complete awareness and power over all material things.

In friendship, you are rather distant and withdrawn. You often seem preoccupied. You have few close ties with people because there are more important things on your mind. Literally, you have no time for friends. Practically no one is on your high level of spiritual development, and this makes for a lonely existence.

In business and finance, you stand an excellent chance of attaining wealth and success. You can go into any business operation and quickly make it show a profit. You can succeed as a leader or subordinate worker, for you are very adaptable and have learned to survive under any circumstances. You may acquire a vast sum of money, but you are charitable and generous; you never hoard or give an impression of greediness or miserliness.

You do not enjoy the manipulations of the huge commercial world, but you realize that money is important to your plans.

In love and marriage, you are a yielding and adaptable individual. You can live harmoniously with any vibration, but a relationship with an 11 or another 22 would be most beneficial and rewarding for you. You are much too practical for the glamorous attraction and excitement of romance. You should marry someone who is on your level, spiritually, emotionally, and intellectually. Otherwise, you will grow bored and restless, drifting away from the relationship in search of your soul mate.

You love deeply but often seem aloof since you are not demonstrative with your affections. Provided you choose a mate who has similar interests to yours, marriage can be extremely rewarding for you both.

Chapter Seven

Determining Your Karmic Lessons

*T*he word "karma" is widely used today and can mean different things to different people. For our purposes in this book on numerology, we will simply define karma as the law of cause and effect at work in our lives. Whether we have lived before, or life is a brief interlude limited to the here and now, the soul or higher mind evolves as time goes by, and we inevitably reap what we sow. If we plant roses in our spiritual garden, we will get roses; and if we plant bitter herbs, that will be our harvest. Past actions affect present circumstances, and we must confront the lessons life expects us to learn.

Although karma is based on the theory of rebirth, it is possible to view karmic lessons in a less metaphysical way. In a numerology chart, they merely indicate the various fundamental experiences of daily living that we must learn and personality shortcomings that we must address in our lives. Regardless of your view, this chapter explains how to identify karmic lessons in a numerology chart and how to interpret the meaning and impact of each lesson.

Numerology recognizes nine karmic lessons, and they correspond to the nine primary vibrations (1-9) as shown in this table:

1. Self-Sufficiency; Independence
2. Cooperation; Diplomacy
3. Self-Expression; Creativity
4. Organization; Efficiency; Progress

5. Moderation; Self-Control
6. Fidelity; Honesty; Loyalty
7. Stability; Analysis; Wisdom
8. Material Mastery; Generosity; Ego
9. Optimism; Acceptance; Compassion

When a chart indicates a karmic lesson is present, it means that this individual will be challenged in daily life to overcome or master the negative shortcomings of that vibration and cultivate its positive attributes. Once learned, the lesson no longer has a material effect on the person.

We can expect to find at least one karmic lesson in most numerology charts. In some charts, we may find two. It is unusual for a chart to indicate more than two lessons. As you might expect, the more lessons you have, the more challenging your life is apt to be.

A numerology chart with no karmic lessons is rarely seen. We might assume this to be a positive—an "old soul" with no major life lessons left to learn. That may often be true, but those who have no karmic lessons are often detached, aloof, and border on a cavalier attitude towards life. It is as if they have mastered every lesson, but in the process, lost their zest for living. They may be cynical, apathetic, or pessimistic, or they may come off as captive commuters on the road of life, looking for an off-ramp so they can go on to whatever comes after this mundane existence.

To identify karmic lessons in a numerology chart, look back to your calculations for determining the Expressive Self. Consider the full name at birth, both the vowels and consonants. Make sure your number assignment for each letter is correct. Then, look for missing primary vibrations (1-9). If a number does not appear at least once somewhere in the full name, that missing vibration represents a karmic lesson.

In the following example, all nine primary vibrations appear at least once, except the number 8. This means that Lisa has one karmic lesson, and it is represented by the 8 vibration.

```
LISA    MARIE    ARMSTRONG
3911    41995    194129657
```

When interpreting karmic lessons in a chart, we treat them in much the same way as the Life Path. The vibration is important, but it probably won't be a major concern every moment of a person's life. Its effects will ebb and flow, re-emerging from time to time as a reminder of a life lesson that must be learned.

Note too that a person who has a karmic lesson is not necessarily doomed to repeat difficult experiences over and over. Once a lesson has been learned, its significance and effect fade. It may bubble up again from time to time as a test or a reminder, but its influence fades over time. Thus, when interpreting a chart, it is possible that an individual will shrug and feel that a karmic lesson is not present in daily living because they have dealt with it already and overcome that challenge earlier in life.

Following are the interpretations of the nine karmic lessons:

Guide to Karmic Lessons

1

This karmic lesson indicates a lack of independence or self-sufficiency in the past; perhaps an inability to stand on one's own feet or relying too much on others. If you have this lesson, you will be prone to avoid decision making or you procrastinate too much. By failing to act or assert yourself, you permit other people to make decisions for you and control your life. Another manifestation of this lesson is an unwillingness to accept responsibility for mistakes or shifting blame for bad luck or your shortcomings to others.

Life will insist that you learn the crucial lesson of independence and self-sufficiency. You will find yourself in "sink or swim" situations where you must stand on your own, think for yourself, and take charge of your affairs. If you fail to do so, life will disappoint you at every turn, and goals will always be out of reach.

To master this lesson and minimize its impact on your daily living, learn to be an individual and develop your inner strength. Become self-reliant. Think for yourself and take responsibility for your actions. Don't let the fear of making a mistake stop you. To err is human! Stop procrastinating—decide what needs to be done to move your goals forward, and do it. Make bold decisions, be courageous and confident. Your new-found independence will be rewarded with concrete results.

2

This karmic lesson portends that you will encounter setbacks in daily life sparked by lack of diplomacy or tact, an unwillingness to cooperate, or an inability to compromise. Until this lesson is learned, it will bring instability in your affairs and difficulty reaching your goals, even when they are close at hand. Friendships and romances will be strained; arguments will erupt frequently.

Life will place you in situations where your goal is close at hand but you must work with others to achieve it. Without a spirit of cooperation, you will encounter frustrating delays and failure at every turn. You must use tact and diplomacy to accomplish your goals, and until you do, opportunities will slip away, forcing you to return to square one and start again. Likewise, your relationships with friends, family, and colleagues, will be strained, and your romances will erupt in discord.

This should not be a difficult lesson to learn. Try to see things from others' points of view in daily living. Maintain an open mind, leave your biases out of it, and work to negotiate an acceptable compromise. Look for opportunities to volunteer your time and interact with others. Make yourself available as a negotiator, peacemaker, or counselor at home, school, or work. Be willing to jump in and help friends in conflict find common ground. Do this until a tactful, cooperative approach becomes an ingrained habit.

Mastering this karmic lesson will greatly improve the stability of your relationships with friends and loved ones as well as your outlook for success in your business or profession. Harmony, stability, and positive energy will flow freely in your day-to-day affairs once you have mastered this lesson.

3

The challenge of this karmic lesson is learning to express yourself and develop your inborn creative abilities. If you are shy and introverted, life will put you in situations where you must learn to become more gregarious and outspoken. If you are hindered by a creative block (such as writer's block), you will need to look inward to identify and overcome whatever is causing it. Fear of public speaking, lack of self-esteem, being painfully self-conscious, and keeping a tight lid on your emotions are shortcomings that indicate this lesson has not yet been learned.

Conversely, some individuals with this karmic lesson go to the other extreme: their creativity is running rampant, and it is so undisciplined and unfocused that it causes them to be flighty, impulsive, obnoxiously outspoken, or their imagination is so overactive that they cannot focus on a project or channel their energy to see it through. If you fall into this group, you must break out of this creative wasteland and apply self-discipline so that you can develop your talents to the fullest. Free yourself from repressive situations in your home life and relationships. Let your artistic temperament shine through and put some color into your life.

You will find yourself in situations where you must express your ideas or utilize your creative abilities to reach your goals. When you retreat into shyness or allow your artistic expression to be stifled, life will make you come out of your shell if you want to accomplish anything.

This karmic lesson can be mastered rather easily by stopping yourself when you repress or hide your feelings—or when your creativity falls into a rut, consciously will yourself out of it. Express yourself! Say what you think, share what you feel, and do not let circumstances or other people dampen your creative potential.

Proactive actions that you could take to master this karmic lesson might include joining a debate club, taking a speech or acting class, seeking a job doing telephone surveys, or signing up to volunteer for a political campaign. Spending a few hours each week writing, painting, singing, or indulging in an artistic talent you enjoy and that requires you to open up and share your feelings with others. You will realize that you are brimming with wonderful creative ideas and can be brilliant at whatever you do.

4

This karmic lesson can affect you in three ways, and several may apply at once: a state of constant disorganization in your life; a tendency to daydream, cut corners, and avoid hard work; and obsessing on minor details and perfectionism to such an extreme that you bog down in trivia and finish little or nothing. This lesson is all about organization, a balanced approach to detail, and efficient use of energy to make progress toward your goals.

Those who have this karmic lesson typically have problems with obsessing over details or glossing over them. They may become preoccupied with minor side issues and fall into a rut, or swing the other way, taking careless shortcuts or making rash decisions to avoid that rut. Either way, they lack efficiency or organization, or both. They invest a great deal of effort into projects but accomplish little, leaving others to mop up half-finished efforts.

As you work through this lesson, life will show you that nothing can be accomplished without organization and efficiency. You will become entangled in loose ends and disorganized confusion as missed opportunities slip through your fingers. Shortcuts will backfire, and you will have to restart at the beginning. Eventually, you will realize that you waste far more energy doing things over or abandoning half-finished tasks than you would by making a concerted effort to become organized and methodically tackle the task at hand, doing it right the first time.

So, the essence of this lesson is simple: get organized! Take a course on efficiency or read a book with tips on how to organize your life. Buy a diary or journal and train yourself to record the details of your daily affairs. Find a happy balance between obsessing over trivia and glossing over major details to reach a hasty result. Make it a habit to work through things one step at a time and move on to the next task only after you have finished the current endeavor and tied off all loose ends.

When you have mastered this lesson and embraced organization and efficiency in your life, daily affairs will run like a well-oiled machine, and you will advance toward your goals with greater ease than you ever thought possible.

5

The number 5 governs physical health, and the challenge of this karmic lesson is to learn and practice moderation and self-control. If you have this lesson, you'll find yourself in situations where you must exercise restraint, avoid risky behavior, and make sensible lifestyle choices. Failure to do so can adversely affect your health and well-being. Overindulgence and clinging to physical sensation are common among those who must learn this lesson, and unwise choices can lead to a cascade of consequences. Without balance and moderation, you can run your physical and emotional health into the ground. There is a tendency to be accident-prone, so dangerous occupations and sports should be avoided.

Mastering this karmic lesson requires a simple and straightforward plan of action: learn to practice moderation and restraint in all facets of life. Avoid over-indulgence; make healthy choices in your diet and other activities. Recognize that addiction in every form—whether smoking, drinking, overeating, drugs, or sex—is easy to fall into and difficult to overcome once these behaviors become ingrained. Keep your eye on the goal of moderation and self-control. The sooner you master this lesson and put it behind you, the happier and healthier you will be!

6

Often called the "relationship vibration," the 6 karmic lesson is mainly concerned with love, marriage, family, and home life. This is the most commonly reported karmic lesson in numerology charts, but it can be challenging to overcome. The problems that must be addressed and the solutions are not as obvious as with other lessons, where a specific problem and the steps to fix it can be clearly identified. This lesson reflects problems with intimacy and relationships, typically involving a lack of honesty, loyalty, or both. The problems may be of your own making, or you could be on the receiving end of others' actions. The potential solutions or remedies are therefore unclear.

While this karmic lesson is unresolved, you will have stormy relationships that end abruptly. Impulsive behavior, hypersensitivity, arguments, and temperamental outbursts can make things worse, sometimes creating a fertile environment for deception and infidelity. Your history of painful relationships may cause you to shy away from intimacy and seek brief, superficial involvements. You'll be prone to wonder whether you will ever find happiness.

To overcome the destructive cycle of emotional turmoil and broken love affairs, you should take a long, hard look at your relationships and objectively identify how you can make them better. A good starting point would be to ensure that they are built on a foundation of honesty and loyalty. While it's true that you can only control your own actions, you can make up your mind that you will be unwaveringly honest and faithful, and if your partner is not, you can move on to relationships with more promise. Likewise, if you find yourself caught up in an abusive relationship, either as the abuser or the victim, end it immediately before you both suffer even more emotional and spiritual damage. Sowing seeds of discord, whether you plant them, water them, or allow them to grow, will only lead to greater misery.

You will know that you've mastered this lesson when you realize that honesty and loyalty in your relationships are essential if you want to maintain mutual love and respect. Once you do move your relationships onto a positive track, you'll be able to stop running away from intimacy and build lasting relationships that will bring happiness and positivity into every area of your life.

7

The 7 vibration signifies wisdom, insight, maturity, analysis, and balance. Those who have this lesson typically find those stabilizing influences are missing or diminished in their lives. Thus, the negative aspects of this vibration such as lack of judgment, instability, vacillation, fickleness, impulsiveness, and reckless behavior have fertile ground to take root.

If you have this lesson in your chart, it indicates that in the past, or perhaps now, lack of judgment and/or impulsive behavior has caused you much grief. You've probably experienced erratic moods and depression many times. If you have a stubborn streak on top of it, chances are you remain in emotionally unhealthy situations long after you should move on, and you may wonder how your life became such a train wreck. If you look closely, you will see that much of your angst has been brought on by your own actions, especially impulsiveness, which can take many forms: acting on spur-of-the-moment desires without regard for the consequences, making hasty decisions without weighing all of the facts; jealousy (or insecurity); harsh words spoken in a flash of anger. All these mistakes and their after-effects can be countered by exercising balance and wisdom.

This karmic lesson can be mastered rather easily with a healthy dose of clear thinking and emotional balance. You have a sharp mind and great powers of observation—use them! Life will continue to put you in situations where you are tempted to react impulsively—so, change how you react and you will change the outcome. Express the positive qualities of the 7 vibration...Stand back, analyze the situation. Make a serious effort to find constructive actions you can take instead of throwing your hands up in despair or resorting to irrational decisions.

Other helpful steps you can take to master this lesson include: learn to rely on meditation, visualization, and other techniques to stay stable and positive in daily life. Read a book or focus your mind on pleasant, positive thoughts. Remind yourself to think, calmly, before you act. It may not be easy at first, but practice makes perfect, and you will empower yourself to unlock your higher potential and enjoy a brighter life of success and happiness.

8

Numerologists associate the number 8 with the vibration of material mastery. It emphasizes success, wealth, fame, and power more than any other vibration. Thus, as a karmic lesson, it centers on ambition, ethics, generosity, and ego. The lesson is simple: learn to control your ambitions and ego, and learn to share your good fortune. The major pitfall to avoid is blind ambition and the morally bankrupt belief that the means justify the end.

Throughout life, you will find yourself in situations where you must choose between what you know is right and wrong. Inevitably, the wrong choice will have painful consequences. At the very least, you will be kicked back to square one and will have to start over. At worst, you will encounter abject failure again and again. The cycle will repeat until this lesson is learned.

You can ease your challenge of learning this karmic lesson by not being so headstrong and insisting that your way is the only way. Develop the attribute of open-mindedness, and carefully consider what others have to say. Likewise, when success or good fortune falls into your lap, be willing to share it with those who helped you along the way, or even with acquaintances or strangers who are trying to overcome their own hard luck stories.

Ultimately, this lesson requires mastering your ego. Ego and generosity are intertwined. If you choose your own material comfort and self-importance over being a decent human being and caring for others, you may amass a fortune, and you might manage to hold on to it, but it will bring you no happiness.

If you have the 8 vibration elsewhere in your numerology chart, such as the Soul Urge or Expressive Self, you will find yourself given positions of leadership and authority. Guard against being a tyrant, a bully, or a self-important know-it-all. If you have a judgmental streak or you are highly opinionated, these ego-driven qualities will bring this karmic lesson back in play, and you may find yourself stirring up hard feelings among colleagues, friends, and family at every turn. Make a concerted effort to be more open-minded and forgiving. Master your ego and you will rise to the lofty heights of success in life.

9

This karmic lesson does not occur often in numerology charts. The number 9 symbolizes universality, human concern, optimism, self-sacrifice, compassion, and completion. It is sometimes called the "finishing vibration," and many numerologists view 9 as an indication of an old soul when it appears elsewhere in the chart. As a lesson, it represents the absence (or repression) of these positive attributes, or expression of their negative counterparts. Either there is a lack of spiritual awareness; too much pessimism and negativity in your thinking, narrow-mindedness, or lack of human compassion. Some people who have this lesson come across as cynical, uncaring, or detached, as if to say, "I'm an old soul and I've learned everything, so why am I here?"

If you have this karmic lesson, you must avoid martyrdom and self-pity. If you have ever been in a dark mood and felt that your life has always been, now is, and always will be unhappy, it is evidence of the 9 karmic lesson at work. Avoid falling into the negative pattern of hopelessness, defeat, and martyrdom when things in life don't go right.

Fortunately, most people who have this lesson are spiritually aware enough to recognize its downsides and compensate for it, focusing on positive endeavors and compassionate interaction with others. If you are struggling with this lesson, make a special effort to reconnect with human beings and rekindle your optimism and appreciation for life. Reawaken your interest in the world. Get in touch with nature and rediscover the joy of life and the majestic beauty of the universe.

Chapter Eight

The Karmic Projection Table

*I*n earlier chapters, we discussed how vowels and consonants in the full name reveal the Soul Urge, Latent Self, and Expressive Self. We learned how to interpret the Life Path and identify karmic lessons. In this chapter, we will analyze letters in the full name from a different perspective, moving from assessing personality traits to identifying numerological trends that affect an individual from year to year throughout life, as reflected in the Karmic Projection Table.

Before we begin this topic, if you have not yet mastered the basics of numerology presented up to this point, review the earlier chapters to reinforce your understanding. The advanced charting method discussed in this chapter requires a thorough grasp of the various numerological vibrations and their meanings.

The Karmic Projection Table reveals trends at work on three major levels of a person's life—physical, emotional, and spiritual—at any point in the past, present, and future. We use the full name to build this chart. Each letter retains its numerical value assigned earlier, which establishes the duration of that letter's effect. For example, "A" has a value of 1, so its duration in the chart is one year. The letter "B" has a value of 2, so its duration is two years; "C" has a value of 3, so its duration is three years, and so on. Following this logic, we can construct a chart by following the simple instructions given below. An example chart follows.

Chapter Eight

Mapping the Karmic Projection Table is a straightforward process, but letters must be entered correctly and then totaled accurately. Interpreting the chart is the most challenging step, but it can yield a wealth of fascinating and potentially useful insights into past, present, and future trends affecting a person's life.

To construct the Karmic Projection Table, it is best to use a sheet of graph paper, as the procedure involves working with multiple rows and columns of letters and numbers. It is easier to calculate totals and evaluate the results when everything lines up visually. If you don't have graph paper, you can use a ruler to draw your own.

On the top row, in the upper left corner of the sheet, write the number "0" which signifies the person's age in the first year of life (birth to first birthday). Working to the right, in the next square, write the number 1. In the next square, write "2", then "3", and so on, extending the chart to whatever chronological age you wish.

For the example given at the end of this explanation, we will use the birth name *Thomas Marshall Dillon*. On the second row, directly below the "0," write the first letter of the first name. So, for Thomas, write a "T" in that square. Because T has a value of 2, write a second "T" in the next square. Never skip over or leave blank squares in the chart.

The next letter in Thomas is "H" which has a value of 8. So, write eight H's in the squares to the right of the two T's that you just entered. Go on to the third letter in the name, which is "O" and has a value of 6. Write six O's in the squares to the right of the eight H's. Repeat for the remaining letters in the first name until you have filled the squares to the highest age that you want to evaluate in the chart.

If you use all of the letters in the first name before you reach the end of the chart, start again with the first letter of the name and repeat until you complete the row to the desired age. Thus, if the first name is short, you may cycle through the letters several or more times in an extended chart that spans, say, eighty years. For instance, the name "Ann" will fill 11 squares (A=1 + N=5 + N=5). So, you will cycle through those letters eight times to construct a chart that spans eighty years.

On the third row, below the letters of the first name, repeat the procedure just described, populating that row with the letters of the middle name. Repeat again on the fourth row using the letters of the person's last name.

When you have finished constructing the Karmic Projection Table, you will have a row of numbers along the top representing the person's age, and three rows of letters below derived from their first, middle, and last name. These letters reflect the Physical, Emotional, and Spiritual trends dominant in their day-to-day life and environment from one year to the next.

Letters on the Physical line reflect major changes in residence, health, material surroundings, new jobs and lost jobs, brief and prolonged periods of financial gain or loss, and other trends of a physical or material nature.

Letters on the Emotional line reveal major influences pertaining to friendship, home and family, love, marriage and divorce, periods of happiness, stress, depression, boredom, grief, and other conditions that may exert emotional and psychological effects.

The letters on the third line reflect spiritual trends at work in a person's life. Many numerologists construe "spiritual" to mean events and influences having to do with creative, intellectual, moral, religious, and metaphysical influences and activities in life. Some treat the letters of the last name on this row as a reflection of karma or universal undercurrents at work from year to year.

Once we have mapped the Karmic Projection Table up to this point, our next task is to add the letters on the Physical, Emotional, and Spiritual lines for each year, much as we did with the Karmic Essence in Chapter Six. Total the three letters shown under age 0, and reduce to 19 or less, or 22. Always reduce 10 to 1. Write the sum in the square directly below the three letters. Repeat for age 1, 2, 3, and so on, until the entire chart has been calculated.

The numerological vibration deduced by adding the letters on the Physical, Emotional, and Spiritual lines for a given year is called the "Projective Essence." It is important because it reflects the cumulative effect of the vibrations at work on all three levels. Thus, the accuracy of a chart depends on your addition being correct. Double-check your math for each value.

The intended result is easier to visualize when you take a look at a completed chart. The example below shows a Karmic Projection Table for Thomas Marshall Dillon, calculated up to age 19.

0	1	2	3	4	5	6	7	8	9	10	11	12	13	14	15	16	17	18	19
T	T	H	H	H	H	H	H	H	H	O	O	O	O	O	O	O	M	M	M
M	M	M	M	A	R	R	R	R	R	R	R	R	R	S	H	H	H	H	H
D	D	D	D	I	I	I	I	I	I	I	I	I	I	L	L	L	L	L	O
1	1	16	16	18	8	8	8	8	8	6	6	6	18	1	17	15	15	15	18

Let's step through this example. At age "0" (birth to first birthday), we see a "T" on the Physical line, "M" on the Emotional, and "D" on the Spiritual, which have the values 2, 4, and 4. So:

2 + 4 + 4 = 10

1 + 0 = 1

Write a 1 for the projective essence under age 0. Next, calculate age 1, 2, 3, and so on, extending the chart to whatever age you wish.

Interpreting the Karmic Projection Table is part science and part art, requiring intimate familiarity with numerological vibrations and a dash of intuition. Each letter of the alphabet has a specific meaning and a range of potentially positive and negative effects on one's life while it is active. The position of the letter in the table must be considered. An "F" on the Physical line, for instance, may have a significantly different meaning than an "F" on the Emotional or Spiritual line.

We must consider how the projective essence for a year may influence nearby vibrations. For instance, if a letter on the Physical line is indicative of emotional discord, and the projective essence for that year also suggests turmoil, the combined effect is intensified. Or, if the projective essence indicates harmony, we must factor that into our analysis, as it might dilute the disruptive effect of the letter on the Physical line or even tilt it slightly positive.

Ultimately, in numerology, we must assess how the various influences blend together to reach an accurate interpretation of the chart. It is like preparing a gourmet recipe or a mixed drink—a little more or less of one ingredient can enhance the taste, or cancel it, or leave a bad aftertaste.

In addition, we must consider nearby letters in the chart, looking back one year and forward to the next. Numerological trends do not suddenly kick in on January 1 and end on December 31. They fade in, gradually build, reach a peak, and gradually subside as new trends come into play. Therefore, what happens in a person's life at age 18 will be influenced to some degree by the trends in play at age 17 and will in turn affect the trends at age 19. We cannot simply slice out a particular year, look at the numbers, and arrive at a forecast. We must view the chart as a fluid record of what has been, what is, and what will be.

Avoid overly simplistic interpretations. If an "A" appears on the Physical line, we know that it denotes change. But while the standard meaning might point to a chance of residence, we can't jump to that conclusion. We need to consider, based on other surrounding trends in the chart, what kind of change is likely. Is it good or bad? Will it be a new job? A new home? A return to college? A million-dollar lottery prize? We make that determination by reviewing the trends on all three lines for the current year, as well as for the preceding year and the year ahead.

The Karmic Projection Table can provide truly remarkable glimpses into mundane and universal currents affecting one's life at any given time. But the accuracy of your forecasts will only be as good as your interpretation of the trends and cycles found in a chart. Practice makes perfect. Over time and with experience, you will learn how to recognize and evaluate numerological vibrations and their subtle meanings.

The following interpretations provide a general meaning for each letter when it appears on the Physical, Emotional, and Spiritual lines of the Karmic Projection Table.

Guide to Interpretation of the Letters

A

On the Physical line:

At all ages, this vibration favors change, which often comes suddenly and without warning. The "A" often signifies the beginning of a major new chapter in life. It can bring change in residence, health, or a spurt of emotional growth. Before age 10, it favors sudden change, relocation to a new home or school, and other life-changing events such as the arrival of a new step-parent or the birth of a sibling. Hence, the "A" can be unsettling for young children, and some will have difficulty adjusting to the new.

After age 10, this vibration favors a one-year cycle of abrupt change. It can bring volatile conditions in the home, a change of residence, a sudden job or career change, and significant changes in family relationships. Unexpected financial gain or loss may occur. When followed by "R" or "N," it hints at a brief but possibly serious period of illness or adverse health. Followed by "I," it can indicate health problems precipitated by emotional discord or stress. Followed by "U," it can indicate a difficult year of financial strain or loss.

On the Emotional line:

When "A" appears on this line before age 10, it indicates a year of sudden and unexpected changes in a child's emotions or outlook, such as those that may result from the death of a close family member or a similar event. New ideas and attitudes take root and flourish, usually out of necessity rather than choice. The changes that occur, particularly around the sixth month (when this one-year cycle peaks) will often have a profound and lasting impact. An unstable or challenging home life is typical throughout this period.

After age 10, "A" favors a one-year cycle of change, often unexpected and affecting multiple areas of life. A change of residence is likely. The familiar is replaced by the new and unknown. New relationships begin and old ones come to an end. Love may blossom, but divorce could be on the horizon to make way for the new. This is a time of discovery, unpredictability, restlessness, and potential upheaval. A mixture of positive and negative experiences will lay the groundwork for the next significant phase of this person's life.

On the Spiritual line:

At any age, "A" on the spiritual line brings a positive and highly beneficial one-year cycle. This period will be brimming with new experiences and beginnings, growth, and insight. Discovery, or deep understanding can emerge after a brief period of chaos or turmoil. Spiritual insights and progressive viewpoints on life take root and flourish under this vibration.

B

On the Physical line:

Before age 11, "B" on the Physical line indicates a period of anxiety, stress, and uncertainty in a child's life. Health issues are likely, such as a colicky baby or a youngster with allergies or other immune disorders. The "B" is not life-threatening; it is more of an ongoing source of chronic health issues and stressful times for parents. The child's physical ailments may adversely impact emotional growth and cause finicky or irritable behavior. Fortunately, this vibration only lasts for two years. It is strongest around the end of the first year and gradually tapers off afterward. In a few cases, "B" in this position can indicate neglect or abuse in the home which can have lasting impacts.

After age 11, this vibration continues to be challenging. It often impacts physical health and may trigger chronic conditions, allergies, physical exhaustion, or emotional stress. There is a tendency for poor nutrition, lack of sleep, and other impacts of self-neglect which can amplify the health-related effects of this vibration. Making a conscious effort to embrace healthy lifestyle choices can help mitigate these pitfalls or avoid them entirely. The "B" vibration does not favor financial gain, and money struggles often occur. Career or job changes may be tempting but could worsen the situation and should be postponed when this two-year cycle peaks, around the end of the first year and the beginning of the second.

On the Emotional line:

When this vibration appears before age 11, it warns of a challenging time. Emotional discord or tension in the home is typical, and poor communication with parents. Misunderstandings erupt frequently, and small conflicts are blown out of proportion. Arguments and hurt feelings that occur during this two-year cycle can have lasting effects if not promptly addressed and resolved.

After age 11, this vibration becomes a more positive influence. An undercurrent of emotional strain will likely persist. An important goal may be delayed or emotional sacrifice may be required, but a new reservoir of inner strength will be discovered. Love and romance are favored, and marriage or a proposal may occur. Difficulties communicating with friends and family persist, because the "B" vibration creates a fertile environment for arguments, misunderstandings and hurt feelings. When it appears on this line between ages 16 and 23, it usually indicates the end of a significant relationship and a sense of regret or loss.

On the Spiritual line:

At any age, "B" on this line has minimal significance, as this vibration mainly affects physical and emotional affairs. It may promote superstitious or narrow-minded thinking or cause one to gravitate toward religion as a stabilizing influence. In some charts, this cycle is associated harboring grudges and a tendency to feel stagnant or stuck in a rut without making progress.

C

On the Physical line:

When "C" appears in this position, its effect is almost always positive and beneficial. It reflects heightened awareness, appreciation of natural surroundings, and favors creativity and discovery. Before age 12, it reflects a positive and inspiring time in a child's life when eagerness, intelligence, and independence are highlighted. After age 12, it reflects an adventurous outlook on life, the blossoming of artistic talents, and a desire to be surrounded by color, art, and beauty. Wonderful creative breakthroughs often occur under this vibration.

On the Emotional line:

In this position, the "C" remains a positive influence, bringing a three-year cycle when life is cheerful and harmonious. Challenges and upsets that might occur are handled in a mature and amicable manner. Love affairs are not usually favored because a person under this vibration usually finds it difficult to be tied down to one person. The "C" is primarily focused on self-expression, experimentation, and freedom.

On the Spiritual line:

Inner growth and self-discovery are indicated by the "C" in this position. There is little or no discord or turmoil under this benevolent vibration, and tranquility prevails. It may signal that bursts of creative energy will be released, and a person might be more intuitive, psychic, and emotionally sensitive. Many of life's difficult lessons that one must learn are avoided during this three-year cycle; but it is not a problem, as everything happens in its own time. Under the bright and inspiring influence of the "C," harmony and happiness are the dominant trends.

D

On the Physical line:

Before age 13, this vibration typically reflects health concerns, tension or turmoil in the home, or a general sense of discord. This is not the happiest vibration. Several changes of residence may occur during this four-year cycle. It favors moving forward with plans, but not all progress will be positive. Physical and emotional exhaustion may occur.

After age 13, the "D" brings long journeys, a job change that may not be anticipated and could lead to brief hardship, and some limited success in career or business endeavors. When followed by "N" or "U," it suggests a necessary and probably unpleasant trip, such as to deal with a family member passing away or some other mishap, usually affecting someone outside of the immediate home.

On the Emotional line:

Before age 13, "D" on this line has no particular significance. It can denote minor, ongoing stress in a child's relationship with one or both parents and spurts of defiance or hurt feelings. Strained relationships are usually resolved quickly and without lasting consequences.

After age 13, "D" suggests a string of tumultuous romances that adversely affect physical health or emotional stability. When "D" is followed by an "N" or "R," this scenario is probable. Followed by "H," this vibration can be troubling. It sometimes appears in charts of individuals who move to escape an abusive relationship. It signals that caution and discretion are advisable, especially mid-cycle as this vibration peaks (end of the second year), when an element of danger may be present.

On the Spiritual line:

Here, the "D" often reflects a four-year cycle of organization and attention to detail, when progress can be made toward important goals. Alternatively, the opposite trend may prevail, with entanglements in chaotic disorganization of one's own making. When the "D" is negatively expressed, little or no meaningful progress is likely to occur during this four-year cycle. Fits of frustration and lashing out at friends and loved ones may occur all too often, causing damage to important relationships. All in all, while this vibration is prevalent, striving for organization and balance in daily affairs will help overcome or minimize its disruptive effects.

E

On the Physical line:

Before age 14, the effect of the "E" in this position will be variable, bringing both positive and negative influences into play. A child under this vibration will experience early development, learning to read or write at a young age. They will express a natural curiosity that may lead them into trouble at times. This is a period of outgoing, gregarious interaction with friends and family; a five-year cycle of adventure and happy memories. But the "E" can also suggest dabbling in physical stimuli, such as smoking, drinking, drugs, or other addictive behaviors which may cause parents some consternation. Stubborn behavior is also emphasized. Sudden change, possibly a move to a new home or school, will probably occur and will deeply affect this individual. Feelings of insecurity, restlessness, and a lack of family structure or roots may precipitate a time of instability and acting out.

After age 14, the "E" primarily affects health and well-being. Its appearance on the physical line in an adult chart often signifies a strong desire or need for physical gratification. Habitual use of stimuli such as alcohol, drugs, or sex for the sake of pleasure is sometimes noted. This vibration may also cause love and sex to be confused, leading to strained or broken relationships. Mood swings and erratic behavior are typical. To flip the negative effects of this vibration to positive, emotional stability, moderation, and self-control are essential and will help this individual navigate through this five-year cycle of adventure and pleasure unscathed.

On the Emotional line:

Before age 14, "E" in this position indicates a child who is hard to manage and difficult to live with. This five-year cycle brings heightened sensitivity, moodiness, and strained relationships, which may cause some parents to worry that their child is out of control. During the first year of the cycle, the youngster may seem aloof and absorbed in their own thoughts, but as the second year unfolds, they will become adventuresome, outgoing, inquisitive, and unruly at times. Many changes will occur. New interests will be embraced, old interests will be discarded just as quickly.

After age 14, the "E" sparks an intense interest in dating, love, and sex which often takes on exaggerated importance. During this five-year cycle, one may become obsessed with the pursuit of adventure and pleasure. Heightened impulsiveness can lead to risk-taking behavior, dangerous sports, and addiction to physical gratification in various forms. Intense but deeply disappointing relationships occur. Passionate love affairs flourish, but don't last long. Endurance, stamina, and courage are on the upswing.

On the Spiritual line:

When this vibration appears on the Spiritual line at any age, it signals a challenging five-year cycle. Impulsive and reckless behavior are typical, and the key to surviving this vibration unscathed or flourishing under it is to learn moderation and practice self-control. This can be an enjoyable cycle, filled with adventure, but only if one remains stable and practices restraint. A tendency for accident-proneness is likely, and rash behavior can exacerbate the risk of injury and other consequences. While this vibration is active, an individual will be drawn to colorful and eccentric people and unusual lifestyles. They will fancy themselves as adventurers, perhaps hedonists, always looking for fun and ready to enjoy life to the fullest. This can be a very happy time in one's life, but without moderation and self-control, thrill-seeking escapades may lead to accidents, addictive behaviors, and misfortune.

F

On the Physical line:

Before age 15, "F" in this position highlights family and portends greater responsibility in the home. As this six-year cycle peaks, tension in the home often develops, brought on by the death of a family member, separation or divorce, or other events that may require a youngster to take on adult responsibilities.

After age 15, the "F" brings a major emphasis on romance. Family and home life take on greater importance as well, often prompted by unexpected developments. A tendency to confuse emotional and sexual love can lead to heartache. A close family member's illness or passing may require assuming increased family obligations. Marriage is favored during this six-year cycle, and "F" on this line often signals a new marriage, the birth of a child, or both.

On the Emotional line:

Before age 15, "F" in this position is typically very positive. Life will be happy, secure, and sheltered. A loving family is indicated. Friends will be made easily during this six-year cycle, and some relationships formed now will last a lifetime. Falling in love at a young age is likely, and one may believe with all their heart that they've met the love of their life. Although this isn't usually the case, the romance will last longer than parents and friends expect. Overall, this will be a happy and enjoyable time of life.

After age 15, the "F" signals a more complicated landscape. Emotions are heightened, and dramatic mood swings are likely. The search for love becomes compelling, but a tendency to confuse love and sex will lead to misunderstandings and hurt feelings. On the bright side, this vibration will bring numerous relationships, so loneliness will never be a problem.

Compassion and empathy will be required during this cycle. This person will be called upon to be emotionally strong, stable, and willing to help those in need. But they must know when to walk away from a situation where they are taken for granted or the other person refuses to help themselves. Close friends will provide a stabilizing influence that will help this individual make the most of this cycle and grow into a beautiful, positive human being.

On the Spiritual line:

At any age, "F" in this position is always a positive. It can counter unfavorable trends on the Physical and Emotional lines to some extent. It reflects a mature, balanced outlook on life and a willingness to accept responsibility for one's actions. An optimistic and enthusiastic approach to daily living will favor inner growth, and major goals can be accomplished with surprisingly little effort because everything will fall into place and work out according to plan. Especially before age 24, and between age 33 and 42, this cycle brings stability, happiness, and tranquility into one's life.

G

On the Physical line:

Before age 16, "G" on this line can make a youngster introspective and difficult for parents to understand or communicate with. Secretive behavior, impulsiveness, and dishonesty bubble up. A rebellious spirit may spark frequent quarrels and hurt feelings, causing the youth to be withdrawn and guarded. In some charts, it signals that a teenager ran away or moved away from home at an early age. Hard feelings linger, and it may take a long time to heal.

After age 16, these unstable conditions are likely to persist and may intensify. Young adults experience sudden infatuation, falling in and out of love frequently. Romances will be intense but brief and breakups painful. Marriage at a young age is quite possible, and teen pregnancy is not unusual. Accidents caused by impulsive or careless behavior may occur, especially mid-cycle during the third and fourth year, so caution is advisable.

On the Emotional line:

The "G" here is a dominant vibration, which means it may weaken positive trends or intensify negative trends on the Physical and Spiritual lines. This person becomes more emotional, hypersensitive, and prone to hurt feelings. Bad judgment and reckless behavior can lead to unpleasant consequences.

Before age 16, the "G" can strongly affect a child's disposition, producing outbursts of temper and erratic moods. Secrecy, resorting to white lies, or outright dishonesty may occur. Although the youth may seem aloof and detached, an emotional inferno bubbles inside and triggers unpredictable behavior.

After age 16, "G" on this line becomes a positive influence. It encourages open-mindedness, optimism, and wisdom. Impulsiveness remains an issue during this cycle, and rash actions may be cause for regret. Love and marriage are highlighted, but this cycle also brings infidelity and illicit affairs. If one falls into this behavior, they may find themselves alone or suffering in a dysfunctional relationship. Life will provide many opportunities to grow emotionally and strive for balance, honesty, integrity, and wisdom.

On the Spiritual line:

At any age, this vibration indicates poor judgment and jumping to conclusions. Before age 16, it reflects a natural curiosity and interest in life, but also a sad, brooding disposition. A deep interest in religion and spirituality is likely to develop and flourish.

After age 16, "G" on this line reflects a heightened focus on spirituality. Deeper empathy develops, intuition grows stronger, and psychic abilities flourish. A fascination with the paranormal, metaphysics, or the supernatural may develop, along with a desire to gain a deeper understanding of life and the universe. Ancient wisdom or Eastern religions may lead to a new world outlook. After age 34, this vibration indicates success and recognition. After age 43, it is a very positive influence favoring an extended period of emotional stability and happiness.

H

On the Physical line:

At any age, "H" in this position favors material expansion and prosperity. Success and leadership are favored during this eight-year cycle. However, this vibration can produce resistance, delays, and frustrating outcomes. A stubborn or opinionated disposition becomes pronounced and may sabotage opportunities. Ego must be kept in check to maintain balance and achieve positive goals.

Before age 17, this cycle can reflect stubborn or headstrong behavior that can have a negative or destabilizing effect on family and home life. Opportunities for learning and growth are lost if one refuses to listen to parents, teachers, and mentors. In some charts, a chronic health condition may develop as this cycle peaks.

After age 17, "H" favors an extended cycle of success, recognition, and leadership. This can be a time of prosperity and great progress. If a new job or career is being considered, now is the time to act. A new business could be started or an important real estate purchase negotiated. A love relationship or marriage may take on added importance during the latter half of this cycle, although new romantic commitments are not favored and should be avoided.

On the Emotional line:

Ego becomes a major factor now. Before age 17, one struggles to be assertive and prove their worth, or conversely, to avoid arrogance and over-confidence. Clashes with parents and friends, provoked by an insistence on being right, are an ongoing problem during these years. A rebellious streak adds to stress in the home.

After age 17, ambition is in the spotlight, and this individual will crave success, fame, and power. Progress can be made on nearly all material goals, but emotional affairs will be strained because "H" on this line typically breeds conflict and misunderstandings. An enemy for life may be made, and over-expressed ego is usually to blame. Learning to control the ego and strive for friendly "give and take" relationships will help avoid the negative aspects of this vibration and assure mutually rewarding outcomes.

On the Spiritual line:

The spiritual self is typically neglected when "H" appears on this line, as this vibration is rooted in ego and the material world. Spiritual thoughts are apt to be viewed as trivial or a waste of time. In some charts, this can lead to dire consequences, because there is a tendency for unethical, dishonest, or oppressive behavior. If these qualities are expressed, misfortune or loss is indicated. Cultivating positive spiritual qualities of tolerance, integrity, and generosity will do much to limit or dispel the negative aspects of this vibration. This cycle often overlaps into emotional affairs, fueling a desire for friends, popularity, recognition, and praise, motivated by an underlying desire for ego gratification.

I

On the Physical line:

The "I" on this line can be troublesome, promoting delays, setbacks, and lost opportunities. Struggling to move forward and going nowhere can lead to physical or mental exhaustion, or both.

Before age 18, this vibration usually reflects tension and discord in the home. A separation or divorce may occur, or a family death, causing instability punctuated by fierce arguments and, occasionally, physical conflicts that disrupt the child's security and self-esteem. In some charts, a chronic health condition is indicated, usually brought on by overtaxed emotions. Relaxing and finding solid ground becomes difficult.

After age 18, the same conditions persist, peaking during the fourth and fifth year of this nine-year cycle, and then subsiding. Material and financial goals are not favored. A job change being considered or plans to start or expand a business should be postponed, especially mid-cycle. This vibration sometimes indicates difficult setbacks such as theft, financial loss, or business closure.

On the Emotional line:

The "I" in this position usually reflects an extended period of conflict, emotional discord, and financial hardship. In some charts, it indicates separation or divorce. Sudden, unexpected change, high stress, and uncertainty abound. While this outlook may seem bleak, the silver lining to the cloud is that changes that occur during the first half of this nine-year cycle will set the stage for better things to come during the last three years. Until then, new jobs, business projects, and relationships are best postponed.

On the Spiritual line:

The "I" is a spiritual vibration, and on the Spiritual line in a chart, it is quite favorable. It does not bring the hardship and loss typical when it appears elsewhere. It signals spurts of sudden change, usually favorable, throughout the entire cycle. Often, changes are preceded by initial delays that test one's resolve to maintain a positive outlook. Then, the obstacles melt away and great progress occurs with leaps and bounds. Despite the flurry of activity, this is a time for embracing the spiritual side of life, letting go of the old, and laying the groundwork for the new.

"I" is one of the "finishing" vibrations associated with the number 9, and change follows a predictable course: we must let go of the old, and the new rushes in. All things in life end, and those endings usher in new beginnings. The first half of this nine-year cycle favors self-discovery and planting seeds of change. The last half will see those seeds take root and grow. New ways of thinking will be embraced, new goals set, new outlooks adopted, but only after the old has been released and left behind.

J

On the Physical line:

Before age 10, this vibration encourages natural curiosity and rapid intellectual development. The cycle is brief, lasting only a year, during which the child will be impressionable, energetic, inquisitive, and a fast learner. They will be sensitive and prone to erratic moods. This vibration favors health, and under its influence, serious illness and injury are unlikely. Life is positive.

For individuals who are born with psychic abilities, their first premonition or other extrasensory experience early in life is likely to occur under this vibration.

After age 10, "J" continues to exert a benevolent effect. It indicates a time of learning new skills, setting new goals, cultivating new ideas. Home and family are highlighted. A new romantic interest may enter and develop now that will have a lasting effect on this person's life. Education, career, business, and money are favorably accented, and a major change made now may bring great success and prosperity in the future.

On the Emotional line:

Before age 10, "J" on this line is a mixed bag. It often signifies a time of discord or chaos affecting home and family. The sudden loss of a loved one or sudden illness of a family member may occur, requiring one to shoulder a greater share of responsibilities in the home. This brief but hectic one-year cycle usually causes a person to develop a more mature, practical outlook on life.

After age 10, the positive effect of the "J" is diminished. It represents a one-year burst of sudden change, which may be quite disruptive. Broken friendships and love affairs are possible, as well as sudden stress over home and family. Arguments and misunderstandings are likely to occur more frequently, and hurt feelings must be promptly mended so that anger and resentment do not linger long after this one-year cycle has ended.

On the Spiritual line:

At any age, "J" on the Spiritual line has little meaning. It is possible that a new way of looking at some condition or concern in one's daily life may evolve, and new or renewed interest in religion, philosophy, or the paranormal is possible. A new habit of taking shortcuts or glossing over important details may surface during this one-year cycle and should be recognized and avoided to prevent careless mistakes.

K

On the Physical line:

When "K" appears on this line, it indicates a time of emotional uncertainty, insecurity, and instability. Corresponding to the 11 vibration, it mostly affects emotional and spiritual affairs. On the Physical line, at any age, it stimulates heightened imagination, self-discovery, psychic awareness, and interest in philosophy, religion, or spirituality. It portends harmonious inner growth. Opportunities to explore new philosophies or to pursue educational goals are highlighted. The downside of this vibration is focusing too much on trivial matters while ignoring larger issues in daily life.

On the Emotional line:

Before age 11, this two-year vibration promotes introspection and solitude. A child will seem more withdrawn and perceived as a loner, introverted, and temperamental. The "K" encourages a highly active imagination and creativity, but the youngster will be insecure and lacking confidence. Mood swings will make home life difficult and cause family members to feel as if they are walking on eggshells. Fortunately, this cycle only lasts two years, and the child will emerge from it more thoughtful and spiritual.

After age 11, the "K" takes on added significance, reflecting self-doubt and lack of confidence. A young adult under its influence may try hard to fit in but will have low confidence or a full-blown inferiority complex. He or she may change goals without explanation or warning. A general discontent with their life and surroundings will persist through this cycle.

On the Spiritual line:

The "K" in this position is quite favorable. During this two-year cycle, much attention is paid to the inner self. Breakthroughs of a spiritual nature can be made, leading to great self-awareness or a deeper understanding of life and the universe. When the "K" is followed by the letters "E," "F," "O" or "V," it indicates an important change is on the way that will have a profound effect on this person's life. The change is usually positive.

L

On the Physical line:

This is a three-year cycle, and "L" on this line is beneficial. Before age 12, it portends good health, creativity, sharp intellect, and a positive environment. A child under its influence will be active, gregarious, sensitive, and artistic. He will approach life as a wonderful challenge.

After age 12, the "L" vibration continues to be favorable, indicating a three-year cycle of material gain, success, and happiness. Health and vitality are favored; illness and accidents are unlikely. Travel may be in the cards, especially during the second year of this cycle when it peaks.

On the Emotional line:

Before age 12, the "L" promotes a positive and well-adjusted approach to life. Artistic talents begin to surface, along with an interest in developing them. Happiness shines in all facets of daily living. A child under this vibration feels loved and secure. He will be free to focus on developing self-esteem, confidence, and innate creative talents. Positive thinking is emphasized. Open and relaxed communication flows among family and friends. This three-year period will be remembered as a happy time in one's life.

After age 12, the "L" brings intimacy and happiness in love. New relationships bloom, and romance flourishes. Misunderstandings are few and far between. Creativity is highlighted, and success will come from artistic talents, whether writing, painting, music, art, or other creative venues. This vibration often indicates a marriage, and it will be long-lasting. This three-year cycle will be a very happy and positive time.

On the Spiritual line:

At any age, "L" in this position is favorable. A three-year cycle, it is a time of optimism, creativity, inner discovery, and enjoyment of life. Artistic talents are awakened and refined. Emotional and spiritual growth flourish. Home and family are stable, although change is in the air. An element of unpredictability is awakening, but it does not detract from the current positive and nurturing environment. Life is pleasant and the future looks bright for the duration of this three-year trend.

This is a good time to evaluate future goals and plans, and give serious thought to constructive steps for achieving them. Major goals can be set in motion now, although one might just think things through and indulge in daydreaming. Projects begun under this vibration are almost always successful. An important life change is indicated during the third year of this cycle.

M

On the Physical line:

Before age 13, "M" in this position suggests a difficult time. Health concerns of a chronic nature are indicated in some charts, usually related to an auto-immune issue, poor nutrition, or anxiety caused by discord in the home. A change of residence is likely, especially near the peak of this four-year cycle. The move will be difficult and leave a residual feeling of being uprooted. Meeting new friends and adjusting to a new school will prove difficult. These effects will linger but eventually subside as the child adjusts.

After age 13, "M" on this line denotes financial stress. In some charts, it signals the onset of a chronic health condition. A sudden and unexpected change of residence may occur, followed by a period of unemployment or unfulfilling, short-term jobs. Major decisions should be postponed during this cycle.

On the Emotional line:

Before age 13, "M" in this position denotes a time when a child seems happy and well-adjusted, but the calm is an illusion. Behind the happy facade, stress and turmoil are brewing. This vibration can stir up feelings of insecurity, lack of confidence, and dissatisfaction with one's physical appearance. It is often indicative of moodiness, impatience, irritability, and perhaps depression. This can be a difficult four-year cycle. A hormonal imbalance may be involved, but often, there is no obvious trigger, and the youngster just seems to drift into an unhappy place.

For adults, "M" is a frequent harbinger of marriage, although tension is in the air. The birth of a child is indicated in some charts. This four-year period is stressful because the energy associated with this vibration is highly emotional and unstable. A new love may appear or an old flame may return. Starting a new relationship now will be challenging but it will bestow happiness down the road. Illicit affairs may occur mid-cycle, and travel is likely.

On the Spiritual line:

At any age, "M" in this position indicates that this four-year cycle will be a challenging time. It triggers emotional instability, self-doubt, and deep feelings of insecurity. One may question their purpose in life or their self-worth. In some charts, we are likely to see evidence of an unhappy relationship that should have ended long ago, but it will drag on for the foreseeable future. There is a tendency for poor judgment and the inability to distinguish good from bad, right from wrong, and this may lead an individual to jump into situations that quickly prove to be mistakes. A positive approach to life and a healthy dose of self-confidence will help maintain equilibrium. Therapeutic techniques such as meditation, rhythm breathing, yoga, and aerobic dance will likewise be helpful.

N

On the Physical line:

Before age 14, this five-year vibration on the Physical line has mixed meaning. It favors a close, loving, and harmonious relationship between child and parents, but it also hints at subtle tensions. Stability in the home could be upended without warning. The "N" can be a difficult vibration because it brings change, often sudden and unexpected, and we never quite know what to expect from it.

After age 14, this vibration indicates frequent change, and it can bring unexpected opportunities as well as unforeseen pitfalls. This is a generally positive five-year cycle, but there will be many ups and downs. In matters pertaining to career and business, the "N" is an "indicator vibration," meaning it can provide insights into what is to come, based on which vibrations are close by. When followed by an "R" or "I", it predicts obstacles and delays; major change and decisions should be avoided. When preceded by "R" or "I", it favors change and important decisions and suggests a favorable turn of events is just around the corner.

On the Emotional line:

Here, the "N" has a powerful influence on matters of the heart. However, it is essentially a physical vibration, so its presence on the Emotional line can be problematic.

Before age 14, it is indicative of a child that is difficult to raise; precocious yet naïve, intelligent, and deeply emotional, subject to unpredictable mood swings. Feelings are easily hurt; lingering resentment can grow out of minor quarrels or misunderstandings. In a few charts, "N" on this line may indicate abuse at a young age.

After age 14, this vibration usually reflects a tendency to confuse emotional intimacy with sexual attraction, which can lead to various problems with partners, from arguments and hurt feelings to disillusionment from expecting more out of a sexual affair than it can provide to outright resentment and broken relationships. In some charts, we may find evidence of codependent relationships forming or ending under this vibration. Falling in love at first sight and a string of short-lived relationships are typical in many charts. This five-year cycle can be difficult because one will search for deep true love, but it is rarely found.

On the Spiritual line:

Here, the letter "N" can suggest romantic loss, either in a literal sense or indirectly, such as a lover moving far away, which ends the relationship, although the love may remain intact. More often, this letter signifies a loss of balance or optimism. One may slip backward on the spiritual progress ladder and become disillusioned with life or uncertain about how to achieve happiness. Much energy is dedicated to soul-searching, but since one is likely to keep repeating the same mistakes and isn't ready to change, time and energy are wasted and no progress is made. During this five-year cycle, little or no interest is shown in spiritual growth. Instead, the focus is on a search for love and gratification that will prove frustrating.

O

On the Physical line:

Before age 15, the letter "O" on this line brings a six-year cycle of harmony and stability in the home. A healthy child, both physically and emotionally, is indicated; illness and accidents rarely occur. This vibration favors intellectual growth, which will give the young person an advantage in school and result in high grades, making their parents proud. A fertile environment for education and growth exists, and learning comes naturally. The "O" instills a thirst for knowledge and an inquisitive, open-minded disposition.

After age 15, this vibration suggests a period of decreased emotional stability. In many charts, a string of romantic and sexual encounters will be found, as much effort is devoted to finding one's soul mate or at least a compatible partner. A powerful desire for intimacy dominates this cycle, and when the individual is not in a love relationship, loneliness may be a strong motivator to find someone new. Travel is favored, and some degree of success in career and business is very likely. An opportunity for leadership will arise and probably a new job that will advance one's career. However, this is not a particularly good time to launch a new business. The "O" in this position rarely portends major upsets, but a restless mood may come and go sporadically, especially during the third and fourth year when this cycle peaks.

On the Emotional line:

Before age 15, this vibration reflects a six-year cycle that is mostly positive and stable. The first year may be challenging and is apt to bring unexpected change, typically a new job or relocation to a new town. Otherwise, a happy home life and loving family environment is typical. In some charts, an undercurrent of financial stress may be indicated, usually stemming from a business setback or loss, and it may be necessary to scrimp to make ends meet. Despite this, the "O" denotes a positive time that favors stability, comfort, and emotional security. A young person under this vibration will enjoy a pleasant, sheltered life.

After age 15, new responsibilities involving family and home must be shouldered, often abruptly. Day-to-day interests may change quite suddenly, and this person may strike out in new directions on the spur of the moment, often dictated by necessity. In many charts, marriage is indicated during this six-year period, especially during the second and third year. The birth of a child, or adoption, is also likely. Despite undercurrents of financial strain, this will be a happy time in one's life. It's a good time to relax and enjoy it!

On the Spiritual line:

At any age, the letter "O" in this position is fortunate. It encourages an extended period of harmony, stability, and understanding. Significant spiritual growth can occur under this progressive vibration. After the first year, a strengthening interest in spirituality, psychic development, the paranormal, or religion is quite likely. In fact, an event related to this spiritual quest will be memorable and could dramatically change the course of one's life. A yearning to explore the mysteries of life and understand the laws of the universe is a hallmark of the "O" when it appears on the Spiritual line.

P

On the Physical Line:

Before age 16, "P" in this position indicates a disruption of family or home life and a general state of tension and unhappiness, often sparked by separation or divorce; but other conditions such as frequent, intense arguments or other conflict may provoke tension. Even under the best circumstances, youth influenced by this vibration are highly sensitive, empathic, and easily hurt by careless words. They are intelligent and love reading. Most express artistic talent at an early age. When their feelings are hurt, which is often, they become sullen and withdraw. Parents must watch for this behavior and keep the lines of communication open at all times.

After age 16, this vibration can stir up feelings of insecurity and make a person quite needy. Falling in and out of love often is the norm as one seeks to feel loved and needed. Promiscuous behavior is likely, motivated by a fear of loneliness. Secrecy, lack of truthfulness, and periods of impulsive behavior, erratic moods, and depression may occur. This cycle can be challenging and at times painful, but it also brings emotional and spiritual growth, adventure, and unforgettable memories that will shape the course of one's life. Emotional maturity and wisdom blossom, laying the foundation for lifelong success and happiness.

On the Emotional line:

Before age 16, "P" on this line signifies a very emotional child who is challenging for parents to raise. He or she will be moody, hypersensitive, and insecure. A reprimand, even a raised voice, stirs up a fear of rejection and feelings of insecurity. The young person possesses strong empathy and will experience the moods and feelings of other people on a deeply personal level, which will prove stressful and sometimes confusing. In some charts, promiscuous behavior is indicated, creating another headache for parents. The task of providing a loving home with rules and boundaries will be a full-time job, but on the bright side, this youngster will grow up to be an amazing, sensitive, and caring human being.

After age 16, the "P" usually sets the stage for an emotionally needy person who falls in and out of love with dizzying frequency. Love at first sight is the norm, and each romance becomes the deepest and surest love ever. Most of these involvements will be passionate but brief. During the third or fourth year of this cycle, one of the most significant relationships in this person's life will occur. How it ends will profoundly affect their future love relationships. Overall, while the "P" is active in the chart, this person will yearn for deep love, but they will be rarely understood. Most of their partners will see them as fiery and intriguing but a hopelessly undecipherable mystery.

On the Spiritual line:

At any age, "P" in this position favors an extended period of spiritual growth. Insights into life develop; wisdom and maturity grow with leaps and bounds. A solitary, introverted temperament sets in as this person experiences periods of quiet reflection and soul-searching. A deep understanding of the self will be gained, but this person may devote so much time to introspection that family and friends worry about their mental state.

Q

On the Physical line:

The letter "Q" in this position signals an eight-year cycle of material mastery that typically favors success, wealth, recognition, and power. When "Q" appears here before age 17, it usually indicates an early interest in money, saving, collecting, and owning things. The young person exhibits a knack for numbers and math at an early age, and as a teen, interest in the stock market, investing, gambling, stamp or coin collecting, and various aspects of business.

After age 17, "Q" on this line is quite auspicious and portends eight years of success and financial gain. Opportunities for leadership and recognition will be numerous. A strong-willed, brave, and innovative personality is indicated, along with workaholic tendencies. Good health is favored, and great strides can be made to obtain or increase wealth, launch new businesses, or expand an existing business. One may embark on a new career. Relocating to a new city for work or business is also likely, especially if "Q" peaks in the chart between ages 26 and 35.

On the Emotional line:

Before age 17, "Q" has a positive influence on emotions. Arguments may arise due to a strong, but misunderstandings are quickly settled, and one learns to fine-tune negotiation skills. Cultivating diplomacy and the power of compromise now will help to ensure success in business and personal relationships later in life. This young person will go through a headstrong and obstinate phase for at least a few years during this 8-year cycle and must learn to be more accommodating to keep friends and popularity.

After age 17, "Q" on this line is challenging. As a primarily material vibration, it can disrupt emotions and cause conflict or tension sparked by an overblown ego. Preoccupation with one's own self-importance can strain close relationships and obstruct progress. Financial difficulty is likely due to lack of money to make ends meet, or because of extravagance, stinginess, or greed leading to loss of friends, opportunities, or prestige. Ego can overshadow positive personality traits, and hard feelings may persist long after this cycle has ended. Romance is neglected, which may lead to a workaholic syndrome, and marriage is not favored until the last few years of this cycle, when the ego is brought under control.

On the Spiritual line:

At any age, "Q" on this line indicates stressful and challenging conditions. Being a material vibration, it is not particularly favorable here on the spiritual level and may cause obstacles, delays, and frustration. There is a tendency to elevate material possessions, money, ego, and the quest for power to the spiritual plane where they do not belong. Pursuing success with blind ambition, believing that the end justifies the means, and resorting to dishonest or unethical tactics to achieve goals will be observed in some (but not all) charts, alienating business partners, friends, and family. A strong sense of integrity, honesty, and fair play can help one to navigate these murky waters. Avoid using unscrupulous tactics to gain recognition and respect, and guard against greed and dishonesty at all times under this cycle.

R

On the Physical line:

"R" in this position at any age means that during this nine-year cycle, one must think before acting and understand that cause and effect can have unintended consequences. Governed by 9, this is a "finishing vibration," so its focus is on completion and endings, whether intended or not. Relationships will be strained and fragile, activities involving future plans will be delayed or cancelled. Stress-related health problems are indicated in some charts. Risky sports and dangerous activities should be avoided.

Numerology teaches us that nothing is set in stone, and vibrations indicate how things will unfold if we do nothing to change their course. With sufficient determination, new business ventures can be launched, new projects set in motion, new relationships begun, as long as one is mindful of the natural current and willing to invest the effort to keep things on course and moving forward. Maintaining a healthy lifestyle and managing stress will keep daily life on a positive track.

On the Emotional line:

Before age 9, "R" here indicates emotional instability, loss, or grief. A child may experience loss and realize that nothing lasts forever. Some charts may reflect the passing of a loved one, or loss of peace and stability in the home due to a traumatic event such as an accident, separation, or divorce. This can cause the child to be overly sensitive, introspective, and withdrawn. A tendency to lash out at disappointment or to cocoon as a way of dealing with unwelcome change may be indicated in some charts.

After age 18, the "R" suggests a time of strained or broken relationships and loneliness. It does not mean that every relationship attempt will fail or that one is doomed to nine years of loneliness, only that it will take more work to keep relationships intact and positive. In romance, a diligent effort must be made to keep the relationship fresh and mutually gratifying and to avoid sliding into inertia, which is the natural state of this cycle.

Relying on the numerous positive attributes of the "R" vibration can do much to help overcome difficulties. Understanding, sensitivity, compassion, and a willingness to forgive can turn adversity into gain. Look to see whether other positive attributes appear on the Physical and Spiritual lines of the chart that may further enhance a balanced and constructive approach to life.

On the Spiritual line:

In this position, "R" is a positive influence that favors spiritual growth. Balance, wisdom, and compassion are highlighted. If a second "R" appears on the Physical or Emotional line of the chart in the same year, any potentially negative effects of that second letter will be diluted or canceled.

Before age 18, this vibration is mostly favorable. It portends nine years of rapid emotional and spiritual growth. A few charts may indicate a period of volatility in the home, loss, or tragedy, but these young people will handle crises with surprising resilience.

After age 18, many challenges will arise throughout this cycle. Projects are delayed or terminated, often unexpectedly, but this individual will be able to look within and find the strength and courage to tackle obstacles in stride and turn adversity to advantage. Emotional and spiritual growth are favored. Having faith that whatever happens in life always works out for the best will enable this person to turn challenges into positive opportunities and make solid progress on accomplishing their goals.

S

On the Physical line:

Before age 10, "S" promotes rapid intellectual development. This one-year cycle will bring a phase of being highly energetic, even hyperactive, naturally curious, prone to erratic mood swings. A feeling of being boxed in or restricted may spark arguments and a rebellious streak. Rambunctious or careless behavior could lead to accidents, so it's important to mellow out during this hectic year. Those who have intuition or inborn extrasensory abilities will likely have their first psychic experience during this year.

After age 10, "S" can be challenging. It brings an intense focus on achieving independence or maintaining freedom. A desire to learn new skills or embark on a new job or profession is favorably highlighted. The challenge will be enthusiastically embraced, but setbacks and disappointment may arise from a restless disposition, a tendency to scatter energy, and a desire to reach goals before the groundwork is laid. Home, family, and romance will be stressful this year, and one's focus should be elsewhere. A major change in hometown residence or marital status may occur.

On the Emotional line:

Before age 10, the "S" is a mixed bag. It often promotes a one-year spurt of sudden, unexpected change, possibly intertwined with stress and discord in the home. Some charts reflect the passing of a loved one or some other misfortune that will require the child to grow up faster and shoulder more responsibilities in the home. The silver lining to this cloud is that the cycle only lasts one year, and a mature, practical life outlook will develop.

After age 10, "S" on the Emotional line indicates a one-year burst of change that is sudden, disruptive, and stressful. A long-established friendship or romance may abruptly end. Misunderstandings erupt with little provocation, giving the impression that everyone around is in a terrible mood this year. Arguments that erupt now have the potential to cause lingering resentment, so disagreements must be resolved quickly and amicably.

On the Spiritual line:

At any age, "S" on this line portends a one-year spurt of remarkable inner growth. A spiritual awakening could occur, or in adults, potential enlightenment. At the very least, a clearer understanding of one's needs, desires, and motivations will emerge. New perspectives and insights on life evolve. Interest in religion, philosophy, or metaphysics blooms. One must avoid the temptation to take shortcuts or gloss over important details now or failure could result and necessitate going back to square one to start over.

T

On the Physical line:

At any age, this cycle indicates two years of hypersensitive emotions, insecurity, and lack of self-confidence. Interestingly, these feelings occur because a burst of creativity bubbles up now, accompanied by a vivid imagination and burning desire to express artistic talents. Individuals under this vibration discover talents never before recognized. Art in its many forms (drawing, painting, music, writing, dance, and so on) is in the spotlight. Flashes of intuition and sudden awakening of the sixth sense occur under this vibration. Interest in philosophy, metaphysics, or religion flourishes. A stable home life and positive, harmonious relationships prevail, despite a tendency for high drama and overreacting to perceived slights. It is important to avoid focusing on trivial matters while allowing bigger issues to slip by.

On the Emotional line:

Before age 11, "T" in this position indicates a child who is shy, quiet, and introverted. Family and friends may perceive them as a loner, insecure, hypersensitive, and easily offended. They will be moody and difficult to get along with at home, causing parents headaches and consternation during this brief cycle.

After age 11, "T" on this line reflects a period of self-doubt and insecurity. The individual tries hard to fit in but is painfully self-conscious and probably has an inferiority complex. Their life goals fluctuate unpredictably, and at times, they seem to change course without warning and for no good reason. This vibration often causes discontent with one's surroundings and life in general.

During the second year of the cycle, a serious and meaningful relationship will probably blossom as a desire for security and roots develops. When followed by the letter "M" or "O," marriage is indicated. When preceded by "M" or "O" a serious relationship is broken off, but only temporarily, and the love will remain intact.

On the Spiritual line:

At any age, "T" on this line is favorable and brings a focus on inner growth and spirituality. A significant awakening occurs. Self-confidence grows, along with a sense of purpose and self-worth. This is a positive time, both emotionally and spiritually. When the "T" is followed by "F," "O" or "X," it takes on special meaning: a major, unexpected event occurs during this trend that changes the course of one's life, nearly always in a positive way.

U

On the Physical line:

Before age 12, "U" in this position portends a three-year cycle of good health, emotional stability, and a positive, loving home. This child is exceptionally energetic, outgoing, imaginative, and creative. Life is viewed as a marvelous challenge.

After age 12, "U" brings three challenging years, complicated by delayed plans, unforeseen obstacles, and scattered energies. A feeling prevails that one is swimming upstream, and that getting anything done requires more effort than the end result is worth. In some charts, these conditions are self-inflicted and stem from a lack of focus, frittering away creative energy, and too little effort concentrated on the task at hand. The "U" favors good health, so this should be a time free of physical injury and accidents. A long trip is indicated when this vibration peaks in the second year.

On the Emotional line:

Before age 12, "U" brings three years of positive energy, stable home life, and happy childhood memories. Artistic talents flourish in a sheltered environment, and the child feels loved and secure. Imagination is supercharged. Relaxed communication flourishes. Undercurrents of tension in the home may develop briefly in the second year of this cycle but will be quickly resolved.

After age 12, "U" favors intimacy and happiness. During their teenage years, new relationships blossom, and in some charts, a lifelong love begins. Quarrels and hurt feelings are infrequent. Creativity is strongly highlighted, and success in artistic endeavors is within reach. When "U" appears in this position between age 21 and 30, a marriage often occurs, and it will be harmonious and lasting. Overall, this cycle may be one of the happiest times in the person's life.

On the Spiritual line:

At any age, "U" reflects three years of creativity and inner growth. Artistic talents are awakened and flourish. Family and home are rocky at times, but a mostly positive environment prevails. The future looks bright. This is a good time to assess goals and future plans. Innovative projects started under the "U" are almost always successful. A major life change for the better may occur mid-cycle in the second year.

V

On the Physical line:

Governed by the number 22, "V" is the vibration of the Master Builder. When it appears on this line before age 22, it indicates four years of good health and emotional stability. There is an interest in education, and the individual may return to school or complete a degree program. A consequential job opportunity comes during the last half of this cycle. In some charts, a life-changing surprise is on the horizon.

After age 22, the interpretation is essentially the same. This is an enjoyable and productive period. Significant financial gain is indicated, especially mid-cycle. New friendships develop that will boost career or business endeavors in the near future. Optimism rises, and success comes easily for those who take an organized, methodical approach. Much can be accomplished during these four years with a minimum of effort.

On the Emotional line:

Before age 22, "V" brings four years of open communication, honesty, intellectual growth, and stability. Self-confidence is on the rise. Romance and affection are favored, and a significant new relationship develops. Life is easy and carefree.

After age 22, "V" on this line brings four years of emotional and spiritual growth. Self-awareness and confidence grow. This is an auspicious time to focus on goals and viable ways to achieve them. New plans can be made with assured success, and major life changes undertaken go well. New friends and business contacts appear on the horizon. Hard work, dedication, and attention to detail will open the door to exciting opportunities.

On the Spiritual line:

At any age, "V" in this position is quite favorable. It portends a spiritual awakening, or heightened self-awareness. In many charts, it reveals that the individual has been held back by some adversity, but now those obstacles crumble and four years of substantial progress will unfold. Seeking out answers or help with future plans and goals is favored. New plans can be made during this time, and new projects set in motion.

W

On the Physical line:

Before age 14, "W" in this position reflects a major life change (or several) in this five-year cycle. A move to a new home or city is indicated, but it may be more destabilizing than expected. Many influences are at work shaping this young person's life. Conflict or other disruption in the home is likely, especially around the third year when the cycle peaks. Some of the effects and consequences of these changes may not be readily apparent.

After age 14, "W" brings change in multiple areas of life that leaves this individual feeling frazzled or exhausted. Finances are strained off and on. Spurts of progress can be made toward one's goals, but the pattern of one step forward, two steps back is apt to repeat often and will prove frustrating. These effects become more evident as the cycle peaks in the third year.

On the Emotional line:

Before age 14, "W" suggests impulsive, headstrong behavior. A tendency for accident-proneness is likely, and parents should make a concerted effort to ensure that the youngster refrains from dangerous activities, including risky sports. He will be naturally inquisitive, and rapid intellectual growth is favored. The parental relationship is strained, sometimes by external factors, and arguments flare as the youngster struggles to achieve a sense of freedom, which often provokes a rebellious streak. These challenging trends gradually subside after the third year.

After age 14, "W" signifies interesting, colorful, and downright strange life experiences. A restless disposition may bring about lifestyle changes merely for the sake of creating new adventures. Such change for the sake of change will bring periods of instability.

Romance is favored after age 23, but this person will probably be content to play the field and avoid commitment. In career and other daily affairs, obstacles and unanticipated delays will be the norm rather than the exception. Worries over money bubble up under the "W," but in many cases, extravagance or being overly generous is at the root of the problem. Maintaining a firm grip on finances and other facets of day-to-day existence is necessary to make the most of this challenging vibration and avoid its pitfalls.

On the Spiritual line:

At any age, "W" can be challenging as it signifies reckless, thrill-seeking behavior and clinging to physical sensation. Inner development is sacrificed and put on the back burner. In some charts, a desire for adventure, partying, stimulation, and experimentation may become so consuming that work, school, even simple day-to-day chores are put off. Fortunately, most people emerge from five-year cycle unscathed and with happy memories they will cherish for life.

X

On the Physical line:

Before age 15, "X" represents a moody, temperamental youth prone to anxiety, insecurity, and depression. Hypersensitivity may undermine physical health. Mental exhaustion and poor nutrition are commonly associated with this very emotional trend. It would benefit this youngster to learn techniques of meditation, relaxation, and stress management early on.

After age 15, this six-year cycle becomes more positive. Education, job training, and developing new skills are in the spotlight, and focusing on major goals now will pay off. Success, financial gain, and recognition are within easy reach. At least one long journey is probable. Love and romance are on a positive trajectory; but "X" here usually portends a string of short affairs rather than a long-term commitment. If marriage does occur, it will likely be tense and short-lived. Emotions are over-charged at times, triggering erratic moods and bursts of high drama. Be on guard during the third and fourth year of this cycle, when anxiety and stress can adversely affect physical health.

On the Emotional line:

Before age 15, "X" reflects a six-year cycle of intense emotions, although it is a generally positive time. A stable, loving home life prevails. This individual is probably confident, emotionally secure, and optimistic throughout this period. However, if the letters on the Physical and Spiritual lines skew negative, the interpretation may flip, bringing instability and tension, perhaps caused by the loss of a family member or other discord in the home. Conversely, if positive influences appear on those lines, the benevolent qualities of the "X" will be strengthened.

After age 15, this remains a generally positive cycle. Love and intimacy are favored. Deep, lasting relationships form; childhood sweethearts often marry when this cycle is present in both charts, and the relationship may well be lifelong. Close-knit family ties and a pleasant, stable home life are indicated. In many charts, the birth of a child is indicated.

During these years, this individual will be perceived as highly sensitive, romantic, and sentimental. Decisions are made from the heart rather than common sense or the pocketbook because this vibration instills a strong desire to be in love. One pitfall of the "X" is a tendency for impulsive behavior. Harsh words or foolish actions triggered by jealousy or insecurity can have profound consequences. In a worst-case scenario, the positive influences of the "X" can be polarized, bringing an unhappy time of separation and loss.

On the Spiritual line:

An "X" in this position enhances spirituality and inner growth. This six-year period is usually a time of insight and self-realization. This individual may seem more introverted than usual, but only because deep soul-searching is going on within. Opinions will moderate; open-minded and tolerant attitudes develop. Intuition is more active than usual, and psychic abilities are apt to surface or become much more active now.

Y

On the Physical line:

This vibration primarily influences emotional and spiritual matters in day-to-day living, so when it appears on this line, it is not particularly significant. Before age 16, it can indicate a shy, introverted temperament, insecurity, or a lingering unhappiness in the home. Between age 14 and 16, it suggests impulsive or reckless behavior while oblivious to the consequences.

After age 16, "Y" becomes a high-energy vibration that can push a person to become more sociable and adventurous. Sudden infatuations are likely, leading to fiery but brief romances. In some charts, "Y" on this line indicates the birth of a child, perhaps out of wedlock, or a pregnancy termination. A tendency for accidents and injury from risky behavior may surface, especially mid-cycle in the fourth year, so a measure of caution is warranted.

On the Emotional line:

"Y" in this position portends a period of increased sensitivity, tension, and misunderstandings. This person is apt to be quite argumentative, opinionated, and stubborn. Before age 16, "Y" reflects moodiness and unpredictable behavior. Frustrated outbursts erupt when things don't go as hoped. Conflicts in the home may flare up, and a lack of honesty or candor can escalate into a serious problem when this youth rebels or insists on having his own way. Living with this youngster in their teen years will be quite stressful for parents at times.

After age 16, "Y" in this position becomes a positive influence. It favors an extended period of independence, optimism, and spiritual awareness. Impulsive behavior remains likely, especially mid-cycle in the fourth year; but a moderating influence will kick in, encouraging good judgment and common sense. Love and marriage are accentuated; but infidelity and illicit affairs may also occur. If one strays into these involvements, this seven-year cycle may become a difficult time of mistakes and regrets.

On the Spiritual line:

At any age, "Y" in this position will challenge a person to make important decisions and choose between relying on good judgment or jumping to hasty, impulsive choices. Before age 16, the "Y" encourages a know-it-all tendency that annoys friends and family. Strong views on religion and spirituality often begin to evolve after the second year of this seven-year cycle.

After age 16, the challenge of making life decisions based on good judgment versus impulsiveness will persist. In some charts, temperamental behavior and lack of confidence may have painful consequences. Individuals with low self-esteem will hide this shortcoming behind a facade of stubborn arrogance and the need to always be right. Some may become workaholics to avoid intimacy. Fascination with the unknown, the paranormal or unconventional religions may develop as life's deeper meaning is sought. Success and prosperity are favored, especially after age 34.

This vibration can be quite positive after age 43, bringing a prolonged period of stability, happiness, and spiritual tranquility.

Z

On the Physical line:

When "Z" appears here before age 17, it signifies an extended period of physical and emotional strain. In some charts, an underlying illness or chronic condition is reflected. Ego soars, and a need for recognition becomes a motivating force. A driving desire for success may surface at an early age, compelling this youngster to excel at whatever he does. An ability to manage money remarkably well may become apparent early on. He will have an affinity for numbers and is apt to be intrigued by business, accounting, even numerology. He will be highly competitive with playmates. More than a few sore losers turn up under this vibration.

After age 17, "Z" can be very positive, bringing a promise of great success. Leadership is indicated. This person's success will be limited only by the amount of effort he is willing to invest in an endeavor—and he will probably expend every bit of energy he has to reach a goal. This vibration favors business ventures, partnerships, import/export, public service, management, and setting new plans in motion. Major endeavors can be begun and seen through to completion. Never admit to limits during this eight-year cycle, and you will go all the way to the top in life.

On the Emotional line:

Before age 17, this can be problematic. The "Z" is a physical and material vibration, so when it intrudes into emotional aspects of life, it can cause tension and resistance. Ego is accentuated, and this youngster may brag and exaggerate incessantly. He will be stubborn, headstrong, convinced that he is always right, and often unpleasant to be around. Being competitive and determined, he must guard against behavior that comes off as overly aggressive or bullying. Some teens under this vibration will not have friends or popularity until they learn to restrain their ego.

After age 17, "Z" has a more positive tone. It usually initiates an eight-year cycle of increased responsibility, which the person will handle well. It also brings leadership opportunities. Being a material vibration, it does not favor romance. Throughout most of this cycle, the person will be preoccupied with career, success, and money. He may feel emotionally detached and uninterested in love and romance, making this an ideal time to focus on career and business. This is a time to enjoy one's success, have fun dating, and postpone long-term commitments until a more auspicious time.

On the Spiritual line:

Before age 17, "Z" in this position has limited effect. It can signify a youngster who has (or will) come to believe that "things" equal love, and the more gifts that one receives, the more he is loved. That attitude, if it exists, will be strongest during the fourth and fifth year of this eight-year cycle. If that peak comes after age 14, it can indicate an unhealthy mindset of believing that popularity and friends can be bought. On the positive side, this vibration favors increased confidence, courage, determination, and natural leadership skills. When these attributes are applied in positive ways, they can set one on course for lifelong success.

After age 17, "Z" on this line can be challenging. Its focus continues to be on success, power, and material wealth, and it sometimes leads a person to believe that money can buy spiritual enlightenment. When the "Z" is negatively expressed, serious ego problems surface. The individual will believe that he is always right; that others around him are fools; and that friends, loyalty, and love can be bought if one has enough money. He may become entangled in dishonest activities, such as get-rich-quick plans, pyramid schemes, and stock fraud. When one falls into this moral quicksand, rude awakenings typically occur during the last few years of this cycle. To avoid the pitfalls of this powerful vibration, one must occupy the moral high ground and avoid the relentless pursuit of success at all costs.

Guide to the Projective Essences

1

This vibration indicates sudden and unexpected changes are on the horizon. Old ways of the past are discarded; the worn are left along the wayside. New ways of thinking develop and diverse viewpoints on life emerge. Erratic and impulsive behavior are pitfalls one must avoid. Energy is scattered; many projects are started but few are finished. Responsibilities are accepted, even though they may be too great to be handled successfully. Mistakes are made, but they are later corrected.

2

Peace, harmony, cooperation, and friendship are highlighted throughout this year. Domestic arguments rarely occur and misunderstandings are quickly settled. Life is easy and pleasant. There may be an inclination toward boredom and monotony. In a few charts, this may suggest a cycle of repression, submission, resentment, and a sense of being trapped by circumstance.

3

Creativity, self-expression, and imagination are in bloom this year. New projects and plans advance, and first steps can be taken to fulfill hopes and dreams. This vibration favors artistic expression, especially in art, music, writing, and acting, which will allow the magic in life to be dramatically communicated to others. Arguments and misunderstandings flare from time to time, but they are quickly resolved with no lasting harm to relationships.

4

This year won't be the most exciting; in fact, it is likely to be monotonous. The focus is on attention to detail, slow and methodical progress, careful planning for the future, and adherence to routine. One may have a sense of being stuck in a rut as this year goes along, and a general dissatisfaction with the state of daily life may surface. The four represents hard work and steady progress, as long as sufficient attention is devoted to details and energy is channeled in a definite and constructive way. Job and career are favorably emphasized this year, and material conditions that have caused dissatisfaction in the past can be addressed and improved upon once the six-month mark in this year is reached.

5

This projective essence highlights travel, change, social interaction, and adventure. Domestic responsibilities are put on the back burner. A long trip is likely this year. It will be important to exercise self-control in one's use of physical stimuli such as drinking, sex, and drugs, as there is a tendency for over-indulgence and addiction under the 5. Thus, moderation must be observed at all times. In some charts, the 5-essence can signify illness or an accident, but recovery will be quick with no lingering effects.

6

There is a strong focus on love, family, and home life under this vibration. In some charts, a new marriage, or childbirth, is indicated. Friends and relatives will demand and expect more of your time than usual. Family arguments and lovers' quarrels will flare up under this vibration. Separation from a spouse because of travel, business or emotional discord is indicated in some charts, but any problems that arise will be resolved before the year ends.

7

This is a time for serious reflection on one's life, introspection, and self-analysis. Important life changes will often be contemplated under this vibration. Some of the changes made this year may seem like mistakes at first, but the outcome will be positive. Impulsive and secretive behavior is accented, so it is essential to think before acting. Have a definite plan and stick with it. A challenging year of emotional turmoil is indicated in some charts, and one will often feel misunderstood. Being honest may not always be easy, but failing to be honest will have consequences under this vibration. Be sensible and discreet. Make a special effort to avoid words and deeds that may hurt or upset others.

8

The 8 vibration signifies prosperity, and this year will bring opportunities for success, financial gain, and leadership. Education, career and business endeavors are highlighted, but emotional affairs may stagnate or be stressful. Guard against over-expression of ego and aggressive or overbearing behaviors, as these negative characteristics could undo much of the good that may be accomplished this year. As long as one remains positive and constructive, considerable progress towards goals can be made, and many important changes for the better will happen this year.

9

Often called "the finishing vibration," the 9 in this position will live up to its reputation. Projects are accomplished, final touches are applied. Unfinished business comes to an end, sometimes prematurely. Plans that were started in previous years but never carried forward are now discarded. Inner reflection and taking stock of one's goals and life in general will be emphasized. Rather than feeling a sense of loss or regret that things are coming to an end, it is better to think of this year as a clearing out of the old in preparation for the new, since a 1 vibration next year will bring significant change and set new plans in motion. Now is a time for making major decisions that will be initiated in the year to come. In some charts, depending on other vibrations present, separation, divorce, the passing of a loved one, and other losses may be indicated. Years governed by the 9 vibration can be difficult, even under the best of circumstances. Remain cheerful and optimistic, keeping in mind that the sun always rises in the morning as night is followed by a new day.

10

(See Number One)

11

Under the 11 vibration, the dual 1's will bring a heavy dose of change, often sudden and unexpected. Keeping up with this fast-paced year will be a challenge, requiring you to be cooperative, compromise with others, and strike a balance in all endeavors. Hunches and intuitive feelings will occur frequently, as though someone had turned on a spigot. Listen to your inner voice, as the guidance it provides will usually be spot on. An unexpected adventure may drop out of thin air, or possibly a new romantic that will have an almost magical or mystical quality to it. When the pace of activity during the year becomes hectic, it is important to stay focused and on top of your affairs. In some charts, losing control or becoming frazzled by the dizzying pace of the year's events may lead to a material setback or loss, usually a loss of money, property, or other assets. This will be an interesting year, perhaps memorable, and much progress can be accomplished.

12

This is a creative vibration that strongly favors self-expression through art, writing, music, drama, and other artistic venues. This year will see new ideas take root and allow major projects to move forward to success. One will feel creative, energized, imaginative, even inspired; but the underlying 3 vibration tends to be unstable, and there will be a tendency to scatter one's energies, lose focus, and go off on tangents that require a lot of energy and produce no meaningful result. A restless wanderlust will crop up periodically throughout the year, and moodiness will be on the rise, stalling progress and making it difficult to get along with others. Arguments with friends and loved ones will flare up more often than usual, often provoked by one's own erratic moods and behavior under this temperamental vibration. Be willing to apologize and make amends to keep important relationships on an even keel.

13

The 13 vibration often portends a year of frustrating undercurrents and going in opposite directions. It is a time of inventiveness and originality, courage, progress, creativity, and artistic self-expression. But these positives will only happen if one focuses more on the details and careful planning than on the goals. Glossing over important details, taking shortcuts, and otherwise failing to follow a careful plan of action will lead to unfortunate outcomes, with great ideas going nowhere and straightforward projects ending in a train wreck. A calm, composed, organized, and steadfastly determined approach that reflects the underlying 4 vibration will help move things forward and enable one to navigate through inevitable setbacks and delays.

14

Adventure, excitement, exploring new places, and trying new things come into focus under this vibration. This can be a wonderful year of social interaction, new friends and experiences, and promising opportunities in all facets of life. But it can be a year of contrasts. Overindulgence can lead to erratic behavior and poor health brought on by risk-taking and addictive behavior. Proper attention must be paid to one's health, not just physical but mental. Self-restraint and moderation will be necessary to ensure that one's hunger for adventure does not rage out of control. Because this is such a high-energy time and so much is going on in one's life, a tendency to ignore friends and family can lead to hurt feelings, misunderstandings, and lingering animosity. A new job, promotion, or other financial gain is likely, but careless money decisions may leave one financially depleted at year's end.

15

During this year, the focus will shift to emotional concerns, and the 15 vibration is apt to make life challenging throughout this time. The 1 (outgoing, energized, bold, independent) and the 5 (adventuresome, fun-loving, thrill-seeking) conflict with the down-to-earth, harmonious, home-loving nature of the 6, which governs this one-year cycle. Problems in relationships can develop unexpectedly. Emotions are hypersensitive, and communication with family or loved one may prove difficult. One may feel overwhelmed by marriage or family responsibilities, and there will be a desire to escape or ignore crucial relationships, which may prove detrimental. In some charts, illicit affairs and deception are indicated. On the other hand, single individuals are likely to find this vibration more hospitable. New relationships can be formed, new commitments made, and it may offer a welcome change from single life. Marriages that occur under the 15 vibration offer a better than average chance of longevity and happiness.

16

The 16 vibration in this position is often associated with introspection, self-analysis, lack of confidence, and unhappiness in love. It can make an individual seem aloof and detached. In some charts, it can reflect a broken relationship, loneliness, or a general dissatisfaction with life. Romances begun now are not likely to end well—sometimes because it's just not meant to work out, and other times, it is this individual's own fault. Their desire to find their true soul mate and passion of their life may lead them into secretive behavior and a series of intense but brief romances. If one makes a serious effort to reduce the 16 to the more positive and grounded influence of the 7 by maintaining stability and avoiding impulsive choices brought on by loneliness, this can turn into a much happier year. Important decisions can be made, as long as one is in a stable frame of mind. Education, career, and finances are favorably highlighted, and directing one's focus primarily to these concerns might lead to a more productive year.

17

The 17 vibration can make this year quite successful for you. Career, business, and money are highlighted. This is a good time to start a business, seek a better job, or make long-term educational plans. You may be reluctant to make major decisions; but if they are long overdue, now is a good time to make the jump. You will be able to accomplish much this year if you set your mind to it and you are willing to work hard for it. Look for opportunities where you can shine as a natural leader, and where you can inspire the trust or confidence of others.

Friendships are favorably highlighted, but romance will be problematic, in large part because so much is going on in your life and when you relax, you'll want to be free to do as you please. You may fall quickly out of love with a partner who tries to limit you or puts demands on your time. In all areas of daily life, avoid the pitfalls of headstrong behavior and thinking that you know everything or that you are indispensable. The 17 sometimes encourages a sense of overconfidence, and falling into that trap can put all the good that you might accomplish this year at risk.

18

The year ahead will be interesting and fast-paced, but the person under this vibration will find themselves often pulled in opposite directions. The 1 denotes independence, change, and beginnings; the 8 brings success in work, business, and finance. Together, they reduce to 9, the "finishing vibration," which brings conclusions and puts the spotlight on the inner self. Thus, one must make sense of situations that favor starting, finishing, and building things. The best approach to this conundrum is to practice the art of going with the flow. Focus on starting new projects and moving present endeavors forward as opportunities arise. Bring old conditions in your life which are no longer necessary or useful to a close as you encounter them in daily life. When the influence of the 8 waxes, which favors education, career, business, and finance, push forward with plans in those areas until you run into resistance, and then refocus on whatever opportunities you encounter next to start or finish things. Throughout this cycle, guard against extravagance or spending money you don't have, and avoid taking shortcuts for the sake of expedience.

Friends, colleagues, and others will likely annoy you as this year goes by, taxing your patience or draining your energy. It would be wise to work alone or with just a few colleagues if possible, and leave socializing for another time. By the same token, your closest friends or family are apt to be more needy than usual and will require your time. Make yourself available to the people you deeply care about, and be patient with them—your other projects will wait for you.

19

During this one-year cycle, the 19 will bring opportunities for leadership and financial gain. With that good fortune will come the test that always accompanies the 19, which is a karmic vibration: will you use your power wisely, or will you abuse it, causing harm or loss (in its various forms) to others. Whenever you make the right choice, you will succeed; and when you do not, your endeavor will crash and burn, forcing you to go back to square one and start over. Likewise, with financial gain, will you use your resources wisely for constructive ends, or will you squander your money or use it to gain unfair advantage over others. You chart your own course in life, for better or worse, under this vibration. A positive outlook on life and towards others will go a long way this year.

22

The 22 vibration presages a favorable year that will reward hard work and attention to detail with great success. Opportunities for leadership are favored this year, and one's efforts and accomplishments will be rewarded. Great progress is possible in all undertakings, especially endeavors related to career, business, and finance. However, because so much emphasis is placed on material concerns, creating an imbalance, personal relationships with family, colleagues, friends, and lovers will probably be strained. One pitfall associated with this vibration often seen in charts is a tendency to cut corners, take shortcuts, and allow the ends to justify the means. This can cause an individual to make careless mistakes with significant consequences, or draw them into shady, dishonest, or illegal schemes. This must be avoided at all costs. Philanthropic deeds are favored during this one-year cycle, and involvement in nonprofit activities may lead to further recognition as well as advancing charitable causes that will benefit many. At its best, the 22 signifies deep concern for the world, human compassion, a desire to make the world a better place.

Chapter Nine

Cosmic and Personal Trends

*H*ave you ever noticed that the whole world seems to be influenced by the ebb and flow of unseen but powerful influences? One year, peace prevails; in another year, chaos reigns. A global economic boom showers civilization with prosperity one year, while acts of crazed violence and war fill the daily headlines in some other year. Many people have noticed that major events and trends align with predictable regularity, waxing and waning from one year to another.

Similarly, you might have observed that a certain month or day is difficult not only for you but everyone you know. You have a grueling day at work and return home that night to discover that your spouse, kids, and neighbors similarly awful days too. Have you ever wondered why life unfolds in such an orderly fashion?

In numerology, we recognize that a cyclical ebb and flow of positive and negative energy can daily living and the world around us. We refer to these unseen but quantifiable influences as "cosmic trends." Using the methods described below, it is possible to pinpoint the precise trends and cycles affecting your life and the world around you at any given point in time. We can identify the vibrations and understand how they affected your life in the past; how they are affecting you in the present, and what conditions lie ahead in your future. Forewarned, you can plan for the future and make these numerological trends work to your advantage.

While this claim might seem extraordinary, the best proof is to experiment with these methods and assess their accuracy and usefulness in your day-to-day living. Before long, you will realize why many people consult numerology for insights into the cyclical trends that influence their lives and the world around them.

When charting and analyzing cosmic trends, three aspects require our consideration:

1) Cosmic Year
2) Cosmic Month
3) Cosmic Day

The Cosmic Year reveals the broader influences at work in the world during a calendar year. Likewise, the Cosmic Month reveals global trends in play during a calendar month, and the Cosmic Day reflects the vibrations prevailing on a given day.

To calculate the Cosmic Year vibration, reduce the current calendar year to a single digit (1–9), 11, or 22. The result is the cosmic vibration for that year. As with all numerological influences that we've discussed thus far, a Cosmic Year trend gradually fades in, strengthening until it peaks in the middle of the cycle, and then it tapers off.

Here is an example using the calendar year 1970:

$$1970 = 1 + 9 + 7 + 0 = 17 \mid 1 + 7 = 8$$

Thus, we see that the Cosmic Year vibration for 1970 is 8.

To interpret the Cosmic Year vibrations, refer to this guide:

Guide to Cosmic Year Numbers:

1

This will be a fast-paced year. Groundbreaking discoveries are made and scientific breakthroughs will be in the headlines. Old theories and concepts are discarded as the new comes into focus. Change is the prevailing wind blowing this year; often, the new and often unusual arrive completely by surprise. Historic new leadership takes the stage, and a mood of hopeful optimism prevails. But change is not always peaceful, and violent upheaval or revolution is common under this vibration. Wars may erupt, but typically, they are limited to regional skirmishes and are quickly settled. People become more concerned with conditions affecting their lives. Interest in politics, religion, self-development, and social justice rises.

As this cycle peaks, it can become chaotic. World economies destabilize and new replaces old, upsetting the status quo and how things have always been. A restless discontent is in the air. New movements sprout and people gravitate to groups that reflect their views, taking stronger or more radical stands. Even people usually regarded as quiet and passive begin to loudly voice their opinions.

The 1 Cosmic Year is important because it sets a trend for the next eight years of this nine-year cycle. If peace is the guiding force in this year, it will persist for another eight years. If war and violence are highlighted, worldwide discord will punctuate the remaining years. The old adage applies here: "What ye sow, so shall ye reap." The 1 Cosmic Year is a time of planting, and the seeds sown will bear fruit in the years that follow.

2

The 2 Cosmic Year brings a time of peace, rest, harmony, and recuperation from the hectic year that just ended. Many world hot spots will cool. Major changes are postponed. Negotiations move forward seeking to establish stability and reconciliation. Social movements continue to flourish and attract new support, but some of the urgency from the previous year has dissipated. On the national front, there is a move for opposing sides to get along and compromise on important issues. Globally, the year will see efforts made to attain a state of peaceful co-existence.

This year is particularly significant for interaction among individuals. Harmony, cooperation, compromise, working out differences and resolving discord in the home are favored. All around, a feeling of hope and happiness begins to take root. Financial stresses are reduced. Disputes in the home and among family and colleagues at work wane. Some of the abrupt change and upheaval from the previous year begins to fade, while other lingering conditions are accepted and people begin to adjust.

Changes on a global scale this year will be limited and not particularly significant. Progress and expansion are sidelined as individuals, communities, and nations focus on learning to peacefully coexist.

3

Under the 3 Cosmic Year, high-energy activity is highlighted and creativity will flourish. Culture, art, and entertainment grab the headlines with far greater frequency than usual. Writers, reporters, biographers, and marketers will flourish under this artistic vibration. The 3 is not especially significant for global politics, trade, or economic conditions; but people overall will seem more carefree, creative, and communicative. This is a year for great ideas to come into being, and for projects to be launched with a bold, original flair. Individuals will notice a tendency for tension in home and family life, punctuated by arguments in which ego and a desire to be free is expressed. Problems that erupt under this vibration are quickly settled.

This year is especially favorable for those involved with artistic endeavors such as writing, acting, singing, etc., for they are at the peak of popularity. Personal finances are on the upswing, and global economic conditions remain stable for the most part.

Community groups and nonprofit charities are favorably highlighted, and renewed attention is focused on nature, beauty, conservation, and environmental protections. People are on the go —travel and entertainment boom under this outgoing vibration.

4

The 4 Cosmic Year is a time for organization, hard work, planning, and attention to detail. Diplomacy and negotiation will be required. Stability prevails, but for some, this will be a year of repetition, doing the same things over and over, and having a sense of being stuck in a rut. Few major undertakings are started or finished—the focus will be on often tedious work that must be done to build or accomplish anything worthwhile. For some, the year will become routine and boring very quickly.

Economic stagnation or contraction will be in the headlines, along with predictions of an upcoming recession. Almost no mention of infrastructure will be in the news, in part because projects started over the past several years are now being built out. The hard work that follows bold plans being announced and precedes major feats of accomplishment must be done. Gridlock in government will develop, and a tendency for stubborn inertia. The 4 vibration promotes strict and narrowminded attitudes which will block progress. Difficult negotiation and compromise will be needed to get even minor things done.

Under this vibration, politics is emphasized in a significant way. Activists begin to clamor for the spotlight; new political groups form. A growing appetite for change is countered by stubborn inertia, and what little is accomplished will be in fits of starts and stops. Labor and healthcare will dominate the news. Workers will begin to lay the groundwork for movements to demand higher wages and benefits.

On a personal level, many individuals will find this year stable but boring and financially stressful. They will be stuck in routine, yearning for something better in their lives, but it won't be attainable under the 4 vibration. One must be content to lay the groundwork for change next year when trends are more amenable. Individuals who will do best this year are those who focus on details, focus on hard work without complaint, and tie off lose ends. Money will be strained, but this is not a good time to go on a spending spree. However, home improvement projects already in progress should be finished before year-end when the 4 vibration will be replaced by a faster-paced tempo and less free time.

5

The 5 vibration brings welcome relief from the plodding, detail-oriented 4 Cosmic Year. This will be a year of adventure, freedom, travel, and socializing. It is a good year to buy a car, take a family vacation that has been put off for quite a while, or upgrade one's lifestyle. Making new friends and spending time with old friends is favored under the gregarious, outgoing 5 vibration.

As this year gets underway, the world will seem like a brighter place. People will seem hopeful and optimistic. Economic conditions will pick up significantly, trade will expand, and global tensions of the past few years will subside during the first six months, although this positive outlook is likely to be short-lived.

Under the 5 vibration, individuals who are more restrained and socially conservative may worry that society has run amok. Many people coming out of the somewhat repressive 4 vibration from last year will be eager to enjoy life to the point of recklessness, and some will spend extravagantly as the focus moves to comfort and gratification. New relationships and love affairs are highly favored. A drop in violent crime often occurs, but also an increase in minor infractions, especially drunk driving and drug arrests.

During the first half of the year, a hopeful and friendly mood will prevail in most places. Come summer, however, the 5 vibration has a tendency to shift to extremes. The remainder of the year could keep the focus squarely on peace and prosperity; or the boisterous and unpredictable spirit of the 5 vibration could draw individuals into excessive indulgence, over-reaction, counterproductive drama, social protests, and possible chaos or upheaval.

6

The 6 Cosmic Year brings abrupt changes in world conditions

and individuals' lives. Nations become hostile, reactionary, and protective of their interests. A trend toward isolationism sometimes occurs under this vibration. Arguments flare and may escalate into open hostility if quarrels are not resolved quickly and amicably. People seem more concerned with themselves and their own needs, often to the point of selfish obsession, which may precipitate arguments and hurt feelings.

Love, marriage, romance, home life, and children are a strong focus of the 6 vibration. This is a most favorable time for marriage; but divorce rates spike as well. Families seek to reconnect and grow closer, although the yearning for closeness doesn't always translate into results. Overall, people are reaching out for human contact, emotional support, and intimacy. Relationships gain new importance. The negative aspects of this vibration can also surface, provoking suspicion, jealousy, and hostility, which can be blown entirely out of proportion.

On a societal level, people leave the adventurous and fun-loving spirit of last year's 5 vibration in the past, becoming more conservative and focused on the more serious challenges of day-to-day living. People will seem more sensitive, more needy or clingy, more affectionate, but moodier and more easily offended.

Children are highlighted under the 6 vibration and will require increased attention this year. Education will be in the limelight as well with new emphasis on building new schools or renovating existing facilities; teaching moral values and social skills; and building healthy parent-to-child relationships. More people will be interested in pursuing careers in education, social work, counseling, and caregiving occupations.

The last three months of a 6 Cosmic Year will sometimes take a turn into hostility, suspicion, argument, and discord, both on a personal and societal level. Disagreements are likely to erupt that could have long-term consequences if not quickly resolved. Diplomatic efforts in global hot spots may falter or collapse. Be cautious, be patient, and strike a conciliatory tone.

7

The 7 Cosmic Year has the potential to be a very good year on a personal level for those who approach day-to-day living with a practical or analytical outlook. On a broader scale, this year is apt to be challenging. Disputes between countries arise and wars erupt without warning. Misunderstandings escalate and hostilities flare, building to a crescendo from May on into the summer months. Secret meetings and negotiations are in play as world powers strive to prevent chaos. Economic conditions flounder.

On a community level, people will seem unusually restless and prone to being hypercritical. Distrust in government grows, and conspiracy theories flourish. The 7 brings a time of analysis and scrutiny, but the insights people glean aren't necessarily accurate or founded in fact. The mood across society grows tense and pessimistic as many begin to worry that their lives may be threatened by a tide of global turmoil. Policy blunders and political missteps lead to further complications and resentment.

On a personal level, disharmony and mistrust are on the rise, especially during the summer and early fall. These months favor emotional instability. Compatibility between marriage partners suffers, and children could be impacted by unstable conditions in the home. Partners may be more prone to secrecy; illicit affairs and brief, unstable relationships flourish. Change comes suddenly, and it might not be welcome or beneficial. Negative attitudes work against the positive accomplishments of the past several years, and impulsiveness can exacerbate the problem. Keeping a level head, remaining balanced and analytical, and striving to maintain a positive outlook from day to day is the surest way to make it through what could otherwise be a difficult year.

8

Although negative trends from the preceding year may linger as the 8 Cosmic Year gets underway, those undercurrents will soon be replaced by a highly productive year favoring financial gain, business, and building wealth. The focus moves from emotional concerns to the material, more mundane aspects of life. Money troubles dissipate quickly, and now is a good time to launch a new business or undertake huge projects.

The wheels of progress begin to turn on an international level. Expansion, growth, and a burgeoning global economy are typical under this cosmic vibration. Global business deals are negotiated with major success, and drastic policy changes are set in motion.

On a national level, the economy recovers. Unemployment declines, and the construction industry booms. People become more focused on their physical surroundings, undertaking home improvement projects and similar activities. The global economy expands and standards of living improve around the world. Industry expands, competition increases to a frenzied pitch, and a glut of new products compete for consumer attention. Outdated products disappear just as rapidly.

Technology advances rapidly, and the infrastructure for future growth is put in place. Unemployment often drops to record lows during an 8 Cosmic Year. Jobs are plentiful, wages tick up, and almost anyone willing and able to work will be able to improve their standard of living and enjoy a favorable period of prosperity.

9

After the frenetic focus on business, finance, and affluence of the previous year, the 9 vibration shifts the focus to emotional and spiritual concerns. For some, this is a time of rest and recuperation from a hectic year of pursuing material goals; for others, it is a time of introspection, alone time, and inner reflection. A few will experience passing sadness as they reflect upon missed opportunities, faulty choices, and what might have been if life had taken a different turn. Those who experience this should avoid becoming caught up in melancholy and depression. Broadly speaking, there will be a tendency to cling to familiar surroundings and routine, and to resist change.

By mid-spring, the material influences of the previous year will have faded, and unresolved issues and problems from the past will resurface and require attention. The 9 is the "finishing" vibration, and loose ends must be tied off to avoid carrying these problems into a new, nine-year cycle. Major change should usually be postponed during a 9 cosmic year, and if attempted, the results are apt to be less than satisfying.

Global conditions are strained under the 9 vibration. Forward progress comes to a standstill, proposed treaties not enacted previously are scuttled, and pundits will warn that the economic expansion of the past year is running out of steam. Trade deals unravel, nationalism resurfaces, mistrust bubbles among nations. The momentum for progress and change fizzles, replaced by a mood of maintaining the status quo. Old treaties are reexamined, and may be rewritten or discarded. New treaties and trade deals are postponed indefinitely.

Among the world's superpowers, economic conditions will tend to deteriorate. The stock market will usually contract and pull back during a 9 cosmic year; governments are stuck in gridlock, and innovation on all levels is likely to stall. Major decisions are put off, which is likely to be problematic down the road, because old problems will be carried forward into the next nine-year cycle.

On an individual level, personal relationships are strained, and some come to an end. This is not an auspicious time to initiate new relationships, although strengthening existing relationships is favored. Likewise, marriages begun during a 9 cosmic year are usually ill-fated; however, existing marital and love relationships can be stabilized and strengthened. Introspection, self-analysis, and spirituality are highly favored, and one can make great strides on these fronts during the 9 year. Religious movements flourish under this vibration, and it is not unusual for people to suddenly take a sudden or renewed interest in their church and spiritual beliefs. Answers to deep and meaningful questions are sought as individuals refocus their attention from the mundane world and delve into themselves.

11

As this cosmic year dawns, the 11 vibration brings extremes, volatility, and unpredictable events and circumstances. It is a time, as the saying goes, to expect the unexpected. Chance encounters can lead to highly lucrative business opportunities or whirlwind romance. But by the same token, conditions that one might view as reliable or take for granted can abruptly unravel just as unexpectedly. This vibration brings dramatic change, both ups and downs, on every level. Some people may sense that a mystical quality is in the air—something truly fateful is about to happen, and indeed, psychic/metaphysical influences are at play during the 11 cosmic year. The progressive and futuristic mingle with the old-fashioned; dreams clash with practicalities. Emotions and material interests tug in opposite directions, causing confusion and uncertainty about one's goals over the longer term.

New understandings can be forged and conflicts resolved, yet such forward progress is often akin to opening a can of worms and releasing even larger conflicts to be dealt with. One must stay focused, calm, stable, and adhere at all times to ethical values to accomplish anything during this year's frenetic activity that sometimes seems to border on chaos.

Global conditions are likewise unpredictable and may prove as elusive as the wind. Great strides can be made in trade and finance, often heralded by a sudden burst of activity; but stable situations can unravel just as quickly. Not surprisingly, the stock market is usually quite volatile during an 11 cosmic year. Conditions change so quickly, no one knows what to expect next.

To truly understand the characteristics of an 11 Cosmic Year, we must realize that the chaotic unpredictability and roller coaster ride that the 11 brings are actually tempered by the underlying primary vibration, which is the calm, harmonious, diplomatic 2. Thus, we must blend the influences described in this passage with the conditions mentioned previously for the 2 Cosmic Year. Understanding this apparent dichotomy will enable us to make the most of the positives we encounter during the year and to avoid most of the downside wrought by the 11 vibration.

22

This is a year of great change. The 22 vibration favors growth, forward progress, building (literally and figuratively), and activity. Nations and individuals apply their knowledge and skills to bring major achievements to fruition. Great discoveries and breakthroughs typically occur under the 22's benevolent influence—advances in medicine, technology, fiscal policies, environmental sciences; changes of all kinds for the benefit of the world.

This year will be filled with hustle and bustle, frenzied work, and there will be little time to rest. The pace is fast-moving, leaving no opportunity for procrastination. Those who stop to ponder for too long will be left behind.

During the 22 Cosmic Year, key decisions and policy changes by courts and governments will have far-reaching effects on every stratum of society, from the richest to the working classes. Old laws are tossed and reforms adopted in their place. Global issues are handled diplomatically; threats of war are put on the back burner.

On a personal level, this year is likely to prove exhausting, physically and emotionally, but that feeling will be accompanied by a sense of satisfaction that life in the coming months will be better. We can rest later, after the time for action has passed. Getting things done, effecting change, and making one's life better and the world a better place should be our uppermost concerns throughout this cosmically important and energized year.

Personal relationships are not particularly favored at this time, simply because the major focus is on other things. Quarrels and disputes are uncommon during these months, and most people instinctively understand that this is a great year—it only comes once every quarter century), and they must work together harmoniously for the common good of all.

As with the 11 Cosmic Year just discussed, the 22 is a secondary vibration, and it operates on the foundation of its underlying primary vibration—the 4. Thus, the attributes and shortcomings of the 4 will be apparent throughout the year as the months go by. The 4 is organized, practical, down-to-earth, sensible, strong; it is the vibration of the builder, the planner, the architect; and these qualities create fertile ground for the 22 vibration's master builder to accomplish great deeds.

The Cosmic Month

To calculate the Cosmic Month number, we follow a two-step process. First, we determine the month number from this table:

January	1	July	7
February	2	August	8
March	3	September	9
April	4	October	1
May	5	November	11
June	6	December	3

Then, we consider the calendar year, applying the rules for the Cosmic Year vibration discussed above: that is, add the four digits of the year together and reduce to a single digit (1-9), 11, or 22.

Let's calculate the Cosmic Month value for June 1974:

```
June = 6
1974 = 1 + 9 + 7 + 6 = 23 | 2 + 3 = 5
6 (month) + 5 (year) = 11
```

Thus, the Cosmic Month number for June 1974 is 11. Here's a second example using February 1980:

```
February = 2
1980 = 1 + 9 + 8 + 0 = 18 | 1 + 8 = 9
2 (month) + 9 (year) = 11
```

The Cosmic Month value for February 1980 is 11.

Use the following guide to discover the numerological trends at work for each Cosmic Month vibration:

Guide to Cosmic Month Numbers

1

New projects; future plans; sudden change; occasional chaos from which order will come; new developments; inventiveness; exploration; courage; original thinking; growth; rapid progress; political exploits; heightened stress; anxiety; adrenaline rush; mistakes caused by taking shortcuts.

2

Cooperation; harmony; diplomacy; global peace, or inner peace; serenity; optimism; joy; family stability; positive outlook; little or no emphasis on money; political calm; reduced global tension; new alliances, treaties, and friendships.

3

Creativity; artistic talents; self-expression; imagination; focus on entertainment; social and cultural enlightenment; kindness; free thought; continued tranquility; focus on artistic media; some expansion and financial gain; emotional overreaction; drama; moodiness; temperamental disposition; flightiness; vacillation; indecisiveness; impulsive behavior.

4

Organization; hard work; attention to detail; solid effort rewarded; job promotion or advancement; new careers; material gain; financial accounting; financial management; negotiation and diplomacy; steadiness; grounded practicality; honesty; dependability; moving existing goals and projects forward; relaxation.

5

Adventure; change; travel; entertainment; excitement; leisure activities; social interaction and mingling; fashion; marketing; advertising; sports; friendship; release from boredom and monotony; global expansion; global trade; politics; fundraising; thrill-seeking; clinging to physical sensation; addiction to stimuli (alcohol, smoking, drugs, sex); reckless behavior; accidents; poor health and/or diet.

6

Fidelity, honesty, loyalty; caregiving, and the social safety net are highlighted; marriage, family, and home life; romance; children (or childbirth); fidelity; domestic responsibility; counseling; moving forward on delayed home improvements; morality, ethics, and strengthening inner character; emotional sensitivity; compassion; optimism; little or no emphasis on job or money; greater likelyhood of arguments and misunderstanding with close friends or loved ones; jealousy and possessiveness; selfishness; global tension and last-minute efforts at diplomacy to stave off regional conflicts; positive outlook on job growth, economic stability, and global commerce. When the negative aspects of this vibration are accentuated: secrecy; deception; scandal; illicit affairs; argument; broken relationships, or divorce.

7

A year of difficult choices, and the outcomes of plan undertaken will depend on whether the positive or negative qualities of the 7 vibration are in play. On the positive side: stability; wisdom; analysis; good judgment; insight; truth; wisdom; justice; integrity; self-respect and respect for others; unexpected journeys; important meetings but uncertain outcomes. On the negative side: conflict and turmoil, both on a global and personal level; distrust; suspicion; broken agreements; moodiness; self-pity; selfishness; depression; delays and aborted plans; situations become more serious and reach the boiling point; conflict between nations.

8

Global trade and commerce favorable; imports and exports rise; new treaties negotiated and signed; big business thrives; expansion; growth; sales; real estate and property transactions. On a personal level: a new job or a promotion; success; financial gain; generosity, and sharing; minor or no focus on emotions and spirituality; avoid egotism, stinginess, self-righteous indignation, and decisions pertaining to relationships and marriage.

9

Public service; nonprofit organizations, charities, churches, and expanding the social safety net for underserved groups; caregiving; nursing; ministry; a tilt toward introversion and inner reflection, psychic development, and spirituality; insight; a search within for answers and self-understanding. The old must end to make way for the new, and some endings stir up resistance; a time to tie off loose ends and finish what has been left undone. On a global scale, unsolved problems must be addressed to prevent rapid escalation of problems in the future; resentment, distrust, and hostility among nations; procrastination and failure to act. Avoid self-pity, martyrdom, and cynicism.

11

Unpredictable outcomes—goals undertaken will tend to turn out much better or worse than expected; a year of fluctuation;

erratic starts and stops; a willingness to cooperate but delays, obstacles and disagreements encountered at every turn; conflict between the old and the new—one or the other must be embraced or no progress can be made. Limited financial gain and a job promotion (or career change) is forthcoming. Intuition and psychic abilities are in the limelight; one looks within for answers and guidance; universal theories and concepts. Avoid the tendency to change direction mid-stream and finish projects before moving on to the next. Cooperation, a diplomatic approach to problem-solving, and compromise will help a great deal to make this year less chaotic and stressful

22

Major change and great tasks can be accomplished this year on a personal level as well as in the global arena. The 22 vibration favors major treaties and agreements; expanded trade; economic growth; prosperity; positive headlines on developing nations. The focus is on peaceful coexistence; environmental protections put in place; progress on climate change agendas; progress on all fronts. On a personal level, this will be a good year of positive change, progress, and reaching major goals. Much can be accomplished by those who invest the hard work to move forward.

The Cosmic Day

The Cosmic Day vibration is derived from the calendar day, month, and year. Reduce each of these three elements to a single digit (1-9), and then add the three results, reducing again to 1-9, 11, or 22. This represents the Cosmic Day vibration.

For example, to find the Cosmic Day vibration for March 27, 1975:

```
Month:    3

Day:      2 + 7 = 9
```

```
Year:         1 + 9 + 7 + 5 = 22 | 2 + 2 = 4
Cosmic Day:   3 + 9 + 4 = 16 | 1 + 6 = 7
```

Thus, the Cosmic Day vibration for this date is 7.

To interpret the numerological vibrations and dominant trends on any given day, refer to the Cosmic Month values above.

Chapter Ten

Personal Relationships

*I*n the course of daily living, we come in contact with a multitude of people: friends, family, co-workers, neighbors, acquaintances, even strangers. We may think that we know some of these people well and can read them like a book, as the saying goes. But is this really so? How well do we really know those who are close to us? What future course is our relationships with those individuals likely to take?

Numerology gives us some handy techniques we can use to discover and analyze the personality and behavior of anyone we interact with in life. These techniques have been discussed in earlier chapters. We can pinpoint an individual's desires, abilities, and current activities; gain a glimpse of what lies ahead on their life path; and discern other vibrations affecting their lives and destinies. With these insights, we might say with a reasonable degree of certainty: "I can read you like an open book."

What's missing from all of this is an easy and reliable way to gauge whether our relationships with others are compatible, and how we might interact with them in day-to-day living. In this chapter, we will consider how numerology can be used to provide useful insights into our everyday relationships. Faults, habits, attitudes, virtues, and shortcomings can be readily discerned using these techniques. The proof is in the doing, and here's your next challenge: try it and see for yourself that using numerology for compatibility analysis actually works!

To perform relationship compatibility analyses, you will need a full numerology chart for yourself and the other person, or the two people you wish to analyze. In addition, you must have a basic understanding of six numerological concepts that we'll be working with in this chapter, described below.

1) *Like/Unlike Numbers:* When you compare two charts and find an identical vibration in the same aspect of both charts, we refer to those as "Like" numbers. For example, if your Soul Urge is 6 and the chart you are comparing also shows a 6 Soul Urge, we refer to that combination as Like numbers. All other combinations are Unlike Numbers. Do *not* reduce either number to make this determination. In other words, if one chart has a 7 Soul Urge and the other has a 16, treat those as Unlike numbers.

2) *Odd/Even Numbers:* In numerology, even numbers are 2, 4, 6, 8, 12, 14, 16, 18, and 22; odd numbers are 1, 3, 5, 7, 9, 11, 13, 15, 17, 19. Always use the values which appear in each chart *without reducing* either number. Note that some numerologists treat 10 as an even number. Since this book directs readers to reduce 10 to 1, we treat it accordingly, and it is therefore an odd number.

Identifying numbers as odd or even does not provide insights into compatibility in and of itself. Rather, it is a step necessary to identify Complements and Opposites, which are described next.

3) *Complements:* When both charts have an even number in the same aspect (such as the Soul Urge), or both have an odd number in that aspect, we view those vibrations as Complements. So, if one chart has a 6 Soul Urge and the other has a 12 Soul Urge, they are Complements. Likewise, if one Soul Urge is 5 and the other is 9, those are Complements.

4) *Opposites:* When one chart has an odd number in a particular aspect, such as the Soul Urge, and the other chart has an even number in that aspect, we view those numbers as Opposites. For example, if you find a 5 Soul Urge in one chart and an 8 Soul Urge in the other, we would regard those numbers as Opposites.

5) *Primary Vibrations* are the single digits, 1 through 9. When the charts you are comparing both have a Primary number in a given aspect, such as the Soul Urge, it has special meaning. When both numbers are odd, or both are even, we treat them as *Primary Complements*. So, a 4 Soul Urge in one chart and an 8 Soul Urge in the other, or a 1 and a 7, are Primary Complements. If the Soul Urge in one chart is a primary number and odd, and the other is a primary number and even, they are *Primary Opposites*.

6) *Secondary Vibrations*: Two-digit numbers above 9 are called *Secondary Vibrations*. When the values being compared in two charts are both Secondary numbers, it has special meaning. When both are odd or both are even, they are *Secondary Complements*. So, if the Soul Urge values are 12 and 22, or 11 and 15, they're Secondary Complements. If one value is odd and the other is even, they're *Secondary Opposites*.

The interpretations below will help you make sense of these terms and accurately analyze compatibility using numerology.

Guide to Soul Urge Comparisons

Soul Urge Match: When two charts share the same Soul Urge, the relationship will likely be difficult and probably unadaptable. Conflicts will flare up frequently, and there is little hope for reconciling differences. A struggle to hold the superior role or gain the upper hand will strain the relationship. These individuals will have an instant, intense attraction, but they have too much in common and will overshadow one another. Their goals are likely the same, but the combination formed is potentially explosive.

Soul Urge Compliments: These individuals will enjoy a practical and down-to-earth relationship. It will be a stable association, but one partner or both may find that it becomes routine and monotonous. While they share a great deal of common ground, they tend to avoid deep discussions or expressing viewpoints. Nevertheless, significant goals can be accomplished. In close contact, there probably won't be many disputes, and misunderstandings will be quickly settled. Both individuals can look to this relationship for a strong sense of security, and they will view each other as very dependable. For those who seek home, roots, and peace of mind, this pairing would be ideal. In business, complements bode well for a successful enterprise, but both individuals will play it safe and take few risks. For the individual in search of excitement and variety, this relationship is apt to be disappointing.

Soul Urge Opposites: One might guess that this association would be unsuitable because there is a constant pull in opposing directions, but from this tension, a wonderful exchange of ideas can occur. There will never be a dull moment, and both individuals will share a great deal of knowledge and experience with one another. There will be arguments and misunderstandings, but that only helps make the relationship exciting and rewarding. A powerful team exists when these individuals work together, and one person's weaknesses are apt to be the other's strengths.

Primary & Secondary Paired: When a Primary vibration is found in one chart and a Secondary in the other, the relationship will have a strong foundation and excellent prospects for success; however, friction will develop, and at times, it will seem like this relationship is a pressure cooker waiting to explode. One person must inevitably lead, and the other must be willing to assume a more passive role. Usually, the Primary vibration is more practical and balanced, and thus more likely to take the lead. The person with the Secondary vibration has much to learn and will benefit greatly by having someone who is dependable and down-to-earth. If both parties can accept the relationship for what it is, the results will be quite rewarding. Much good can be accomplished.

Secondary Complements: This association will be difficult and volatile. Goals and desires conflict, and little progress can be made. Communication often will be strained or non-existent as two Secondary vibrations are by their very nature unstable. Arguments will flare and be hard to settle because neither person will be able or willing to invest the patience required to make this relationship succeed. However, if great effort is invested and both individuals are willing to make sacrifices, this could be a mutually rewarding association. Secondary numbers have strong needs and powerful emotions. Through give and take, a meaningful relationship can be built in friendship or business. In romance, however, this association will be particularly difficult.

Guide to Latent Self Comparisons

It is important to know how two people will interact when their latent abilities are factored into the equation. In some relationships, similar or dissimilar abilities might be mutually beneficial; in others, mismatched abilities could spell disaster. Use the below guidelines to compare compatibility of this aspect in two numerology charts and draw your own conclusions.

Latent Match: When two people share the same Latent Self vibration, embarking on any relationship expected to be long-term is ill-advised. These individuals will be highly competitive, argumentative, and prone to frequent quarrels. Both may feel that the other is not adequately supportive, or that they must make unacceptable sacrifices to keep the relationship going. This could easily devolve into a one-sided relationship and lead to much resentment in one or both individuals. Both will be driven by a desire to prove that they are more capable of accomplishment or success than the other, and one or the other must yield or the relationship will self-destruct. This numerological pairing offers little opportunity for change, progress, or expansion.

Latent Complements: This relationship will be built on a solid foundation of mutual respect and a desire to achieve common goals. The relationship will likely be long-lasting, and it could be one of the most important associations either or both will have in their lives. Sometimes efforts will be duplicated and wheels will be spun without progress, but overall, these individuals will work well together. Many common interests are shared, and there's little or no competition for dominance. Both parties will be grounded, they will exercise self-control, and they will share pretty much the same goals, or at the very least their objectives will complement each other. Together, they can accomplish great things.

Latent Opposites: This relationship will be challenging. At times, these individuals will question why they are associating, and they will look at each other as being from different worlds. They have few common interests or goals and nothing to hold them together when faced with adversity or challenges in daily living. In some cases, however, particularly in business, if these individuals can establish enough mutual interest, the association could be successful. One person will be proficient in some things, while the other will excel in other areas, creating a dynamic, powerful combination that will lead to great accomplishments. In emotional relationships, however, this pairing is ill-advised.

Primary & Secondary Paired: This relationship is likely to be unpredictable and potentially volatile. The Primary vibration is more grounded, while the Secondary vibration lacks stability and thrives on creative dreams, which are sometimes unrealistic daydreams. If both individuals are willing to put effort into working together, they can achieve much. The major red flag for this relationship is a lack of communication. The Primary native will find it difficult to understand the moods and whims of the Secondary native, who may feel stifled and grow flighty when confronted by practical viewpoints and down-to-earth ideas or advice.

Secondary Complements: This may be a vexing relationship with constant friction, pulling in opposite directions, and jockeying by both individuals to impose their viewpoints or will on each other. Neither is likely to have the stability or the will to lead the other or to build a healthy foundation for day-to-day interaction. Both individuals are moody, changeable, and prone to flighty or impulsive behavior. Relationships of this nature tend to burn bright for a little while and then burn out rather quickly.

Guide to Expressive Self Comparisons

After desires and abilities, the third factor we must consider in numerological comparisons is the Expressive Level. So, now we will give weight to what both individuals are actually doing in life. We use the same rules for comparison as previously described.

Expressive Match: When two individuals share the same Expressive Self vibration, a relationship would have the potential to be very beneficial for both. They are going in the same direction with the same basic goals in life. They can help each other achieve their highest aspirations. However, they must not allow their day-to-day interactions to devolve into situations where one takes advantage of the other to get ahead. Another downside to this association is that both individuals share many or most of the same faults and weaknesses, which could work to their detriment, igniting bitter arguments when they are in close quarters. In love and marriage, this association is best avoided, but in business, if both parties make the effort to get along well, the resulting partnership could be lucrative, perhaps even inspired.

Expressive Complements: This pairing brings with it quite a bit of tension, but it can be overcome if both individuals make the effort. They must have a sincere desire for the relationship to work, or it will never take root. Quarrels will be frequent, but if disputes are quickly settled and both parties strive to maintain open, honest communication, most of the negative pitfalls that could arise in this relationship may be avoided.

Expressive Opposites: This pairing offers fertile ground for a solid, productive relationship, as long as both individuals are willing to give and take, and they embrace sharing responsibilities. There is much of a beneficial nature that could come from this association, but look closely at both charts to assess whether the other vibrations at play are likely to favor cooperation or could lead to stubborn obstinance. If the latter, this will be a painful association for both individuals, and one best avoided. Each will insist on having their way, often at the expense of the other, and nothing positive will come of this.

Primary and Secondary Paired: The pairing has good and bad points worth noting. The Primary vibration has qualities, especially emotional, which are necessary to the success and well-being of the Secondary. As long as the former is willing to assume the role of parent, best friend, trusted advisor, or to otherwise take the lead, while at the same time being able to recognize and appreciate the creativity and uniqueness of the latter, this relationship will be excellent. If not, things will quickly go off the rails, and the association will likely end with lingering resentment.

Secondary Complements: This relationship will be fiery, and the wise will keep in mind that more often than not, fire burns. A great amount of turmoil can be expected in this association. There may be a tendency for one person to take advantage of the other, or even to become abusive or oppressive. A person with an Expressive secondary vibration is usually very sensitive and can't handle criticism or an overbearing personality. They need kindness and compassion, a good friend, and sound advice. When they don't get the support they expect, they may become angry or bitter and strike back. When both people in a relationship share this same temperament, usually neither can provide what the other requires, and the end result is the blind leading the blind off a cliff.

Guide to Karmic Essence Comparisons

The fourth aspect that we must evaluate in numerological comparisons is the Karmic Essence, which provides useful insights into the overall level of compatibility between two individuals, and the strengths and weaknesses of a potential relationship. As we've discussed previously, the Karmic Essence offers a composite of the vibrations shaping desires, abilities, and present course.

Karmic Essence Match: Two people with the same Karmic Essence will have an innate understanding and sense of purpose in a relationship. If business partners, they will feel as if they're cut from the same cloth; in romance, they will be convinced that they are soulmates and have lived and loved one another before. Despite this wonderful synergy, the relationship may be quite intense to the point that it becomes unbearable for one person or both. Under the surface of their similar temperaments and shared goals, an element of instability is present that can lead to friction. The Karmic Essence and the qualities of each vibration must be carefully considered to discern whether a relationship is worth pursuing or should be avoided. Harmonious vibrations, such as 2 and 6, will produce better outcomes. If any hint that disloyalty, intolerance, cruelty, or abuse may come into play (in either chart), this association could be lethal and should be avoided.

Karmic Essence Complements: This is an excellent foundation for compatibility in business, friendship, and love. The relationship will be harmonious and constructive, and great things can be accomplished. These individuals will share common beliefs and goals, and they're on the same level of spiritual development. As long as they are willing to cooperate and pursue their goals on equal ground, this association will be mutually rewarding.

Karmic Essence Opposites: This is not a favorable foundation for any kind of relationship, whether friendship, business, or love. There is little or no common ground, and both individuals will be intent on pursuing their own goals, seeking different life experiences. Progress is ordinarily a positive thing, but when these individuals move forward with their lives, this relationship will eventually disintegrate. With each step forward, they put more distance between them.

Primary and Secondary Paired: Although difficult, this combination offers one of the best prospects for success in friendship, business, and romance. The Primary vibration will be the more solid and dependable partner, helping to keep the person with the Secondary vibration from flying off on tangents. In turn, the latter will prove fascinating, fun, and inspiring, leaving the former feeling magnetically attracted. This association will see friction and many sparks, but chances are good that the relationship will endure and may even grow stronger as difficulties are put in the rearview mirror. The greatest challenge of this relationship will be learning to understand one another. Once this is accomplished, very little will disturb what will probably grow into a deep and profound relationship.

Secondary Complements: This usually spells trouble. These two natives will be drawn together, and they'll feel a strong bond, but it is often a bond of sadness, loss, or regret shared by people who have experienced great unhappiness and are searching for something to hold onto in life. Such codependency does not favor stable or gratifying relationships. Moodiness will be a constant problem with both individuals; tempers will flare, loud arguments will erupt, and hurt feelings or resentment will take root. For those who are determined to make this relationship work, they must remember that the greatest threat to its longevity will be a loss of communication. However, if the parties involved are sufficiently devoted and stubborn enough to persist, a deep and perhaps even lifelong association is possible. Much progress, particularly in terms of emotional development can result, but it will take determination to hold the relationship together, and if a real desire doesn't exist on both sides from the start, it's best to move on.

In conclusion, as is the case when you interpret other aspects in a numerology chart, always remember that nothing is ever set in stone. Numerology provides signposts. It can help us anticipate and plan for things likely to happen when particular vibrations are at play. but ultimately, human beings have free will, and we choose our paths on the road of life.

Whenever you are in doubt about a compatibility analysis, refer back to earlier chapters and re-read the interpretations of the various numbers. For example, if you are unsure about a Soul Urge comparison, review the chapter on the Soul Urge and carefully weigh the positives and negatives associated with each vibration that you find in the charts you are analyzing. Drill down until you are able to form conclusions that make sense to you intellectually and that "feel right" to you on an intuitive level.

Chapter Eleven

The Elements

The final important fundamental of numerology involves the numbers and their respective elements. To determine what kind of relationship will exist based on this, identify the element for each chart you wish to compare and consult the interpretations below.

For comparisons, always use the most dominant chart as a lead. For example, if the Karmic Essence in your chart is 8, and the Karmic Essence in the other chart you are comparing is 2, we know that 8 is dominant (leadership) and 2 is passive (cooperation). So, you would use your own element as the primary key.

Number Correspondences to the Elements

1	Fire
2	Water
3	Fire
4	Air
5	Fire
6	Earth
7	Water
8	Earth
9	Air
10	Fire

11	Water
12	Air
13	Air
14	Earth
15	Water
16	Earth
17	Fire
18	Air
19	Earth
22	Water

Compatibility of Elements

Earth + Fire: Strict and regimented; difficult
Earth + Water: Friendly and cooperative
Earth + Air: Argumentative in close association
Earth + Earth: Quite physical—does not favor emotions

Fire + Fire: Bad—close relationships will be very strained
Fire + Water: Repressive—does not favor trust or intimacy
Fire + Earth: Strict and regimented; argumentative
Fire + Air: Excellent—these elements are complementary

Water + Fire: Repressive—not good in any sense
Water + Water: Slow, unmoving. Likely boring or tedious
Water + Air: Good—these elements are complementary
Water + Earth: Excellent in all senses

Air + Fire: Excellent—these elements are complementary
Air + Water: Good—these elements are complementary
Air + Air: Instability—does not favor close associations
Air + Earth: Argumentative in close association

Chapter Twelve

Sample Chart & Analysis

Let's construct a sample numerology chart and analysis for a fictitious person named Maryjane Sue Lyons, born Nov. 16, 1979.

```
        M A R Y J A N E   S U E   L Y O N S
        1 7 1 5     3 5     7 6
```

First Name	1 + 7 + 1 + 5 = 1 4
	| 1 + 4 = 5
Middle Name	3 + 5 = 8
Last Name	7 + 6 = 1 3 | 1 + 3 = 4
Soul Urge:	5 + 8 + 4 = <u>1 7</u>

```
        M A R Y J A N E   S U E   L Y O N S
        4 9 1 5     1     3   5 1
```

First Name	4 + 9 + 1 + 5 = 1
Middle Name	1
Last Name	3 + 5 + 1 = 9
Latent Self:	1 + 1 + 9 = <u>11</u>

```
        MARYJANE   SUE   LYONS
        41971155   135   37651
```

First Name	4 + 1 + 9 + 7 + 1 + 1 + 5 + 5 = 33
	3 + 3 = 6
Middle Name	1 + 3 + 5 = 9
Last Name	3 + 7 + 6 + 5 + 1 = 22 | 2 + 2 = 4

Expressive Self: 6 + 9 + 4 = <u>19</u>

Let's double-check our calculations before moving on. First, reduce the Soul Urge and Latent Self to single digits. Then, add the two numbers together and reduce to a single digit. The sum must equal the reduced Expressive Self number. Otherwise, you have a math error and need to recheck your calculations.

Using Maryjane Sue Lyons' chart as an example, the Soul Urge is 8 and the Latent Self (11), which we reduce to 2. Add these values (8 + 2 = 10) and reduce as needed (1 + 0 = 1). The result (1) should match the Expressive Self (19 reduces 1 + 9 to 10, which again reduces 1 + 0 to 1). It's a match, confirming our math is correct!

```
              November 16, 1979
```

Birth Month	1 + 1 = 2
Birth Day	1 + 6 = 7
Birth Year	1 + 9 + 7 + 9 = 26
	| 2 + 6 = 8
Life Path:	2 + 7 + 8 = 17
	| 1 + 7 = 8

Our final step is to determine the Karmic Essence by reducing the Expressive Self and Life Path to single digits, then adding those two numbers together, reducing to a number between 1 and 19, or 22. Always reduce 10 to 1. We also examine the first, middle and last name as a whole, and if any vibrations are missing, we note those as karmic lessons.

```
Expressive Self    1 + 9 = 1 0 | 1 + 0 = 1
Life Path          8
Karmic Essence     9

Karmic Lessons     2 , 8
```

Sample Chart Analysis

Soul Urge (17):

Maryjane is a born leader. She is strong-willed, resourceful, and capable of handling major problems, but the small issues of daily life often trip her up. She will channel all her energy into reaching her life goals but overwork herself to exhaustion. She is organized and efficient but not always dependable. She wants to be recognized for her abilities and accomplishments but doesn't respond well to being ignored. Throughout life, she will likely craft numerous get-rich-quick schemes that rarely pan out because she doesn't put enough into the planning stages.

Maryjane can be impatient and doesn't like having to wait for the results of her efforts to materialize. She tends to seek instant gratification and may be just as impatient with friends and family. She expects them to live up to her standards, which often leads to disappointment because most people are not as focused or driven as she is. She must guard against narrow-mindedness, intolerance, and being judgmental or she will alienate people whose support she needs to accomplish her life goals.

Latent Self (11):

Maryjane will be best suited to professions in social welfare, counseling, religion, politics, and occupations concerned with justice and social change, such as working in politics, advocacy, journalism, law, and the nonprofit sector. She is intuitive and spiritual, and she has a great deal of empathy. She wants everything in life to be fair, and injustice greatly upsets her. She often gets involved in the problems of other people, and sometimes, she is drawn into shady dealings because she tends to be too trusting and believes everything has some good in them. Her family and friends sometimes worry about her being naïve, and their worries may be warranted.

Maryjane has the potential for leadership and may find herself at the forefront of social or reform movements. She will find herself placed in positions where she must make decisions of a monumental nature that will affect the lives and fortunes of many. She is conscientious and always puts forth her best effort. She should avoid the pitfall of moping over past mistakes.

Expressive Self (19):

Maryjane is good at producing new ideas and devising ingenious plans to develop and promote new inventions and theories. She should be at the head of her own business, or she should be a freelancer where she can work on her own, since she finds it difficult to confine her thoughts to limits set down by others.

Life Path (8):

This Life Path accentuates success, wealth, power, and leadership. Maryjane will be placed in situations throughout life where she is called upon to take charge and lead. Many people who share this vibration tend to be introverted, possibly even shy or reserved. But this demeanor will not take her very far toward her goals, and she will find more success by developing her leadership potential and personality traits that empower a strong leader.

Great financial success and recognition are likely on the 8 Life

Path. However, Maryjane can be her own worst enemy and must guard against flashes of temper, or conversely, feelings of inadequacy; otherwise, valuable opportunities will be lost. Life will move along for her with great leaps and bounds, and then she will drift into a period of stability and hard work, laying the foundation for her goals and accomplishments. At times, this will leave her feeling like she is stuck in a rut. She should realize that any major goal worth achieving takes time and effort, and she must patiently work through the steps to reach the end result. As long as she remains focused and maintains a positive, optimistic outlook, every goal will be within her reach.

Karmic Essence (9):

The quest for emotional fulfillment and happiness is never far from Maryjane's thoughts. Deep down, she craves security, a happy home life, and roots. She yearns for someone to love deeply who will love her just as deeply in return. However, life will frequently give her reminders that she cannot be tied down. Her mission in life is universal—she belongs to no one person but to the world.

She is philosophical, open-minded, and deeply spiritual. She is flexible and can adjust to any condition or circumstance that life throws at her. Occasionally, she will resist change and cling to the familiar comforts and people around her. After painful reflection, she will make the difficult choices that are required to fulfill her greater purpose in life.

Under this Karmic Essence, Maryjane will have many friends, and she will put considerable effort into trying to maintain deep and meaningful relationships with them all. She is basically honest and loyal, and she does not like liars, hypocrites, hurtful gossip, or two-faced people. When she finds such an individual among her friends, she can easily turn against them, cut them off, or treat them in a rude or dismissive manner until they get the message and leave her alone. Despite her yearning for deep friendships, they don't usually last very long, and in a matter of months or a few years, she will let go and move on to a new circle of friends and acquaintances. She will attempt to keep in touch with old friends by phone or letters.

In business, Maryjane will be better suited to working under superiors rather than trying to lead her own business or organization. She may lack the hard-nosed qualities necessary to start and grow a lucrative enterprise.

In love and marriage, she will gravitate toward partners who are sympathetic, thoughtful, gentle but strong, generous, and concerned about the problems and injustices in the world. In any relationship, she will thrive only if given total freedom of thought and action. If her partner tries to own her or hold her back, her romantic attraction and affection will fade, and she will drift away.

The 9 Karmic Essence can be challenging for those who are determined to find happiness in love or to enjoy a happy family and a home with a white picket fence. All things in life are possible, given that we have free choices in every facet of our lives, but 9 is called the "finishing" vibration, and it can be stressful on love relationships. Separations are likely to occur, although the love may remain intact.

Karmic Lessons (2, 8):

The karmic lesson of 2 indicates that Maryjane will face setbacks in her daily life due to a lack of diplomacy or tact, unwillingness to cooperate, or inability to compromise. Until she learns this lesson, she will experience instability in her daily affairs and difficulty reaching her goals, even when they are within reach. She will encounter strained friendships and romantic relationships, and arguments will erupt frequently.

Life will lead Maryjane into situations where her goal is close, but she must work with others to achieve it. Without a spirit of cooperation, she will encounter frustrating delays and setbacks at every turn. She will need to use tact and diplomacy to accomplish her goals, and until she does, opportunities will slip away and she will have to start again from square one. Likewise, interactions with friends, family, colleagues, and love partners will be strained.

This karmic lesson should not be difficult to learn. Maryjane must try to see things from others' point of view as she goes through her day. She should maintain an open mind, leave her opinions and biases out of it, and work to negotiate a happy compromise. She might look for opportunities to volunteer her time and interact with others, or make herself available as a negotiator, peacemaker, or counselor at home, school, or work. She should be willing to jump in and help friends or family members in conflict find common ground. She needs to continue doing this until a tactful and cooperative approach becomes an ingrained habit.

Mastering this karmic lesson will greatly improve the stability of her relationships with friends and loved ones as well as her prospects for success in her business or profession. Harmony, stability, and positive energy will flow freely in her everyday affairs once this lesson has been mastered.

The 8 karmic lesson is associated with material mastery and accentuates success, wealth, fame, and power more than any other vibration. Thus, as a karmic lesson, the 8 indicates lessons involving ambition, ethics, generosity, and ego. The lesson is simple: Maryjane must learn to control her ambitions and ego, and learn to share her good fortune with others. The most significant pitfall to avoid is blind ambition and the power-driven view that the means justify the end.

Throughout life, Maryjane will find herself in situations where she must choose between what she knows is right and wrong. The wrong choice will have painful consequences, and the cycle will repeat until this lesson is learned.

Maryjane can ease her task of overcoming this karmic lesson by not being so headstrong and insisting that her way is the only way. She must learn to be open-minded and carefully consider what others have to say. Likewise, when success or good fortune falls into her lap, she must be willing to share it with those who helped her along the way, even passing acquaintances. Ultimately, this karmic lesson is one of mastering ego. It requires the realization that ego and generosity are intertwined. If she chooses her own comforts and self-importance over being a decent human being and caring for others, she might amass a fortune and manage to hold on to it, but it will bring no happiness.

If Maryjane has an 8 vibration elsewhere in her numerology chart, such as in the Soul Urge or Expressive Self, she will almost certainly find herself given positions of leadership and power throughout life. She will need to guard against being a tyrant or a bully. If she has a judgmental streak, is highly opinionated or narrowminded, these ego-driven personality traits will bring this karmic lesson back into play, and she may find herself stirring up hard feelings among colleagues, friends, and family at every turn. She should make a concerted effort to be more open-minded and forgiving. By mastering her ego, she will rise to the heights of success in life.

A Few Observations:

In this example chart, we see considerable emphasis on business, leadership, and success. If Maryjane decides to pursue this road, her chart reflects many positive qualities and influences that will help ensure her ultimate success. There is recurring advice in several places that she should focus her interests on areas which involve social or reform movements, schools, churches, legal and counseling services, or other nonprofit endeavors.

One red flag stands out in the Karmic Essence, in which the notation appears that Maryjane would be better off working for someone else rather than in her own business because she is not hard-nosed enough to make tough decisions. Rather than viewing this as a contradiction, we can think outside the box and see various possible solutions. For instance, she could focus on the nonprofit sector, where caregiving and compassion are typically a greater focus than a drive to make a profit and expand a business.

We also see a potential conflict in several places where Maryjane could be pulled in opposite directions, seeking a business career on the one hand and a yearning for the intimacy of marriage and a family on the other. Again, rather than viewing this as a negative, it would be more helpful to stress prospective workarounds: for example, if she found the right marriage partner who is supportive of her career and has the patience to deal with a hectic life of long work days, weekend meetings, travel, and other likely demands on her time if she were to become a success story in the business world.

As we've discussed before, numerology is not a system that provides certain glimpses of the future or that we can use to make infallible predictions. Instead, it provides signposts along the road of life and enables us to identify the influences at work around us and take a creative approach to problem-solving. By learning to interpret these signposts, we can make the best of every opportunity that comes our way in life.

Chapter Thirteen

Sample Projection Table & Analysis

*I*n this chapter, we will construct a sample Karmic Projection Table. This advanced chart requires a person's full given name at birth. For this example, we will continue with the name used in the previous chapter: Maryjane Sue Lyons. Refer to Chapter Eight (*The Karmic Projection Table*) for details on how to make and interpret this chart for yourself and others.

Karmic Projection Table for Maryjane Sue Lyons:

0	1	2	3	4	5	6	7	8	9	10	11	12	13	14	15	16	17	18	19
M	M	M	M	A	R	R	R	R	R	R	R	R	Y	Y	Y	Y	Y	Y	Y
S	U	U	U	E	E	E	E	E	S	U	U	U	E	E	E	E	E	S	U
L	L	L	Y	Y	Y	Y	Y	Y	Y	O	O	O	O	O	O	S	L	L	L
8	1	1	14	13	3	3	3	3	17	18	18	18	2	18	18	13	15	11	13

20	21	22	23	24	25	26	27	28	29	30	31	32	33	34	35	36	37	38
Y	J	A	N	N	N	N	E	E	E	E	M	M	M	M	A	R		
U	U	E	E	E	E	E	S	U	U	U	E	E	E	E	E	S	U	U
Y	Y	Y	Y	Y	Y	Y	O	O	O	O	O	N	N	N	N	S		
17	11	13	17	17	17	17	12	14	14	14	16	16	14	14	14	1	9	13

In the chart above, we find that Maryjane had a period of poor health during her early childhood. A serious illness is indicated at age 3. After that cycle wanes, conditions stabilized and her life became a time of positive self-expression. She exhibited many flares of creativity.

From age 10-15, we see that the focus shifted to her inner life and spirituality. Maryjane was moody, introspective, aloof, and highly sensitive. She experienced a major disappointment at age 13-14, indicated by a cycle of cooperation suddenly reverting to a state of emotional withdrawal.

Maryjane's 16th and 17th years were stable and productive. She achieved some of her key goals at the time. (The 17 Essence blends harmoniously with the Soul Urge in her chart.) However, these years also brought strong tendencies for secrecy and hiding her activities from parents and possibly her friends. Having developed emotionally early in life, it's likely that Maryjane goes through a difficult period of promiscuity. She has at least several, and probably numerous, secret romances, making this a turbulent and trying time. At 18, she turns to perseverance and hard work. At 19-20, her thoughts turn to home and family (the 15 Projective Essence indicates a cycle of domesticity).

At age 22, new conditions develop and Maryjane's life changes course, probably not in a beneficial way. The "A" on the Physical line is followed by "N," which is a difficult combination. She drifts back into a period of introversion and emotional conflict, reflected by the 9 Projective Essence and the 9 Karmic Essence in her chart. This is a time of growing focus (and perhaps obsession) with emotions and love. This cycle peaks at age 24.

From 25-28, Maryjane's life path will bring her to opportunities for leadership, but the stress and anxiety she experiences as a result will most likely undermine her health, indicated by the appearance of "N," an emotional vibration, on the Physical line. Work, self-direction, and a spirit of cooperation with others during these years can create a favorable environment in which she can accomplish much. Significant financial gain, or a major career boost, occurs at age 25-26.

From age 28 and up to the end of the partial chart we've created, Maryjane's life settles down and takes a very positive turn. The anxiety and stress impacting her health now fade, and the "E" provides positive support. But her romances continue to work to her detriment. The "U," usually a favorable vibration, is not so favorable when it appears on the Emotional line, and Maryjane will again be prone to secretive behavior, introspection, and dark moods. We can be fairly certain, based on the 15 Projective Essence, that the stress she experiences during this period will arise from her love and family relationships. However, she will be able to nip problems in the bud before they become crises by understanding the 15's powerful influence on emotions. She must guard against negativity taking root, and in this way, she can for the most part neutralize the potentially negative influences often encountered under this vibration.

As we have said before, in numerology, the simple fact that a particular vibration appears in a chart does not necessarily mean that its impacts, for better or worse, will come to fruition. Number vibrations are not a reflection of destiny but rather indicators of what trends will be in play at any given time in our lives. When positive trends prevail, we must capitalize on them to achieve success. When difficult vibrations are waxing, we can consciously guard against them and be relatively immune to their effects.

Conclusion

If you have followed the tutorials in this book, you should now possess a solid grasp of the basics of numerology. We have examined how personal and cosmic vibrations affect everyone alive, and how nothing in the universe is truly random. We've explored the positive and negative attributes, the strengths and weaknesses, the pros and cons of each vibration and how they may influence us in our day-to-day living.

If you have constructed a few numerology charts for your friends or family, you've probably been surprised by the accuracy of your charts and the insights they provide. Numerology not only reveals a person's outward characteristics but also their innermost desires and abilities, and the life experiences which await them.

Now all that remains is for you to apply these useful techniques and insights to everyday life. Consider ways that you can harmonize your Soul Urge desires with your Latent abilities and your present course in life. Identify your best qualities and build on them; pinpoint your shortcomings and turn them into positives. Discover creative ways to rewrite your song in life so that every note will blend into a perfect melody.

Most of all, refine your understanding of numerology so that you can interpret the signposts revealed to you and follow their insightful guidance to make your life truly wonderful. To do that is to master life and the universe.

www.ingramcontent.com/pod-product-compliance
Lightning Source LLC
Chambersburg PA
CBHW012207090526
44583CB00022BA/2932